BEYOND DEPRESSION

02. 22. 98

To Fr. Fred,
with fondness and appreciation.

Andy

Beyond Depression

A PRACTICAL GUIDE FOR
HEALING DESPAIR

ANDREW CANALE

ELEMENT
Rockport, Massachusetts ● Shaftesbury, Dorset

© 1992 Andrew Canale

Published in the USA in 1992 by
Element, Inc.
42 Broadway, Rockport, MA 01966

Published in Great Britain in 1992 by
Element Books Limited
Longmead, Shaftesbury, Dorset

Designed by Roger Lightfoot
Cover design by Max Fairbrother
Typeset by Colset Pte Ltd
Printed and bound in the USA
by Edwards Brothers, Inc.

British Library Cataloguing in Publication Data available

Library of Congress Cataloging-in-Publication Data

Canale, Andrew.
Beyond depression : a practical guide for healing
despair / Andrew Canale
Includes bibliographical references.
1. Depression, Mental—Religious aspects—Christianity.
2. Spiritual healing.   I. Title.
BV4909.C36   1992
248.8'6—dc20   92–1033
ISBN 1–85230–341–7 (pbk.)

TO RICHARD PAYNE

When my friend is away from me, I am depressed;
nothing in the daylight delights me,
sleep at night gives no rest,
who can tell about this?

The night is dark, and long . . . hours go by . . .
because I am alone, I sit up suddenly,
fear goes through me . . .

Kabir says: Listen, my friend
there is one thing in the world that satisfies,
and that is a meeting with the Guest.

The Kabir Book (Robert Bly, translator)

CONTENTS

ACKNOWLEDGMENTS

As with any effort of this kind, several people have helped in various ways to bring this book to life.

Thanks to: Morton Kelsey, Madeleine L'Engle, my editor Richard Payne, Frances Scribner, John Vara, and Walter Wink who read various versions of the manuscript and urged me to find my own voice. To Carol Maage at Element for helping me get the book in final form.

Thanks to: all the unnamed people who come to my office and teach me how to struggle with isolation and depression.

Thanks to: my wife Kay and kids Sarah and John.

INTRODUCTION

Depression is a cry in the soul that says something is dreadfully wrong. Everyone knows depression. We are all touched by it. It is that vague feeling that something is amiss. It is that wish to do nothing, to vegetate, to die because nothing matters. It is that anguish that our lives mean nothing, that we are isolated beings who are born alone and die alone. It is that awareness that there is something malignant in life, something beyond our little selves that seems bent on destroying us, on crushing our lives into dust.

Shakespeare wrote: "Gold lad and girls all must, as chimney-sweepers, come to dust." Is this the whole story? Do we smell in our souls our decaying beings? Are we locked into an awareness that we have no ultimate value? If so, is it any wonder that we all know depression?

I believe that human beings have ultimate value. That each of us is uniquely important in the cosmos. That the universe is purposeful and is moving toward a great fulfillment. That a Great Lover beckons to each and to all, and longs for us to come home to join in the feast of life. We who feel like dust are life itself. We are God's celebration of the goodness of being. This is what I believe in the depths of myself. And what I long to believe.

But something is amiss. Something in us cries out that though we long for this it just ain't so. It can't be. Look at the emptiness of our lives. Look at the economy. Look at all the death and destruction in the world. Look at the smart bombs that zero in on targets and blow them to kingdom come. Look at the skinny arms and bloated bellies of starving children. Look, look, look, cries our desperation. How can we speak of feasts when bellies are empty?

But why bother filling bellies if we are ultimately nothing? But if we are nothing, why are we so touched? Why this outcry in our hearts, begging us to listen, to see, to do something for God's sake to help these sufferers?

But there is too much suffering. It overwhelms us. We cannot solve these perennial problems. They defeat us. We should give up. There is something deep inside each of us that despairs when we look at our world.

But. Isn't there also something deep in us that cries, "No! No! I won't stand for it! It is all wrong! I can't let that child starve!"

What if this cry is God? What if our aching and sense of point-lessness is God grabbing hold of us and saying, "There *is* more! This isn't all there is. I need you to help. Whenever a child is starving, I am starving and so are you. Your belly pain is spiritual hunger, your soul's resonance with that child's suffering."

We are all connected to each other and yet some of us never know it. Some of us are suffering in most awful and obvious ways. Others are suffering in most awful and hidden ways. When a child starves, God weeps and wails. When a soul goes dead, God moans and groans.

Dare we believe such a thing? Dare we see depression as not only a sign that something is dreadfully wrong, but as a painful move-ment toward something that is wonderfully right?

You probably recall the childhood game Hot Potato in which each child throws the imaginary potato to another child as though it is burning hot. The object of the game is to be not holding the potato when the signal is given because the one left with the potato is eliminated. Interesting game. It playfully pulls kids in because kids don't like pain. And they don't like being eliminated.

Neither do we. We don't like being burned. There is a natural, built-in mechanism that causes us to jerk our hands away from extreme heat. To avoid getting hurt. And elimination represents the final hurt. It has powerful connotations for adults. It conjures death and even murder. Exclusion.

Do we live in a cosmos that eliminates us? That tosses us out when we are eliminated? Are we so unimportant to life that we are just food for worms? Are we finally just part of a food chain that survives because it eats itself? Creatures on our way to dust? Such questions are depressing. They bring us back to where we started from, to depression.

"Ring around the rosey, pockets full of posey, ashes, ashes, we all fall down." This childhood ditty comes from the time of the Black

Plague when people by the thousands were dying in the streets. From the beginning of our lives, even unknowingly, we are fed images that starve us, given messages that say we are only dust.

But something in us reacts, cries "No!" Most of us have become so deaf to this cry that we feel it as only an ache, a poignant reminder that something is missing.

Something *is* missing. We are right. Our depressions confirm it. But we are looking for solutions in the wrong places. We have to be or we would have found the answer by now. Something is missing and it must have great value. Why else would we feel so hungry? Why don't new cars, new houses, new jobs, and new spouses satisfy this hunger?

I'll tell you what I think. Most of us are profoundly isolated in our deepest selves. The cry in us is a cry to be seen, to be met. Do you know the feeling (I hope you do) of meeting another person with whom you can be whole, be totally yourself? Is there something in you that responds and longs to capture that feeling, which is as elusive as the mythical unicorn who could only be caught by a virgin?

I want to come to the problem of depression with a virginal attitude. For you cynics, let me add that virginal does not equal naive. I want to meet depression in a fresh new way. I want to rename depression as an experience of soul to be entered rather than as a problem to be solved. The problem of depression is that we have *made* it a problem. We have not seen it as a statement of soul, an announcement that something is wrong that wants to be made right, that something is missing that wants to be found.

Depression is a clue thrumming in our beings. It is a way to find what is missing. We must pass through it or die, become dust. Suicide is a tragic capitulation to the belief that we are dust. It reminds us of the utter seriousness of our virginal endeavor. We have everything to lose.

I am writing this book because I want to share with you. I want to suggest the possibility that Love calls me and you and us toward meaning. Love that is real is personal. I remember a "Peanuts" cartoon in which Linus is expounding to Charley Brown how much he loves humanity. When Lucy bumps into him, Linus screams at her that she is a clumsy oaf. When Charley Brown reminds him of what he has just proclaimed, he answers in effect, "Oh I do love humanity. It's people I can't stand."

Loving ideas, ideals, and abstractions doesn't bring us into communion. Sharing who we are is what brings us to communion. Each of us is a mysterious picture of mysterious Love. Each of us uniquely portrays a possibility for being.

In my counseling work I daily hear cries of depression. People are in an agony of isolation. Can we try together in this book to share with each other? Can I tell you what I believe about healing love and why I believe it? Will you open yourself to my questions and invitations to share with me? Can we let down the barriers between us that are killing us? Can Love touch each of us so that we both leave this book transformed? I know it is a possibility. May it be so.

1

HALLOWEEN

There are times in life when we are overwhelmed by the power of life itself. Halloween, 1970, was such a time for me, when old definitions and understandings dissolved and a new perspective on life began to emerge. I have written about Halloween elsewhere. I have spoken about it in lectures and in workshops. I have pondered its meaning in silence. I have discussed its meaning with close friends. After twenty years, I think I am beginning to see its significance for my life.

And yet, I feel shy once again as I begin to retell the story, for it is a tale of fear and vulnerability. I ask myself if I'm being exhibitionistic. Shouldn't I keep such experiences to myself? But if I do, the book ends here for I have little to say about depression if I avoid this. I forfeit our possible connection.

THE FEAR OF RISK

at least likely

At the same time, there is a risk. What happened to me may push you away. You may not want to enter into dialogue with me. But that is the risk of living. Unless we can find ways to be who we are, we are destined, we are destining ourselves, to isolation. Better to be isolated because we showed ourselves than because we refused to play. And if you hear me, if my story touches you, it may invite you to speak. With that, you, too, have another opportunity to risk rejection, to risk acceptance.

Risking acceptance is a curious notion. Perhaps deep acceptance is more fearful to many of us than isolation. Why else do we isolate our true selves from others? Why aren't we running up to people and yelling our stories at them, falling on our knees and begging them to hear us?

We enter strange territory with these questions. There are all sorts of reasons not to cry out to people. Decorum for one. What would the world look like if people were throwing themselves around this way? How would you even get to work? How would you handle their desperate needs? And what about your needs? Would you pull the other person to her feet and then throw yourself before her? "Listen to *my* woes! Listen to *my* pain! Please! Help me! Help me! Have mercy!"

It begins to sound like a tale from a holy book. Only in a holy book a saint, or the Buddha, or Christ would respond by helping the person somehow. Why aren't we helping others? Why isn't someone helping us?

"Uh, excuse me," you may be muttering by now. "You were going to tell a story about Halloween."

Yes indeed. And look at the contortions I'm going through trying to get there, trying to avoid it, trying to limber up my muscles so that the story can flow. Maybe now I am limber enough to leap into my story. I'm like the sweaty kid standing at the edge of the pool of cold water. I want to jump. I'm ready to. Here goes.

THE ONE WHO CAME TO HALLOWEEN

I was a senior at the University of Notre Dame in 1970, full of promise and questions. Time to explore these questions was running out. Graduation would soon be upon me and after it the real world. Now was the time to get those questions answered. Several friends of mine had taken a popular course by theologian John Dunne called, I think, Philosophy of Religion. Dunne was renowned as a brilliant, challenging, and exciting teacher. I entered his course with real curiosity. He would answer my questions.

But quickly, I was in over my head. His evocative survey of the history of religion put before me new pictures and possibilities that distressed and troubled me. The account of the god Krishna's conversation with Arjuna in the Hindu Bhagavad Gita particularly upset me. In the story, Krishna tells Arjuna that it is all right to kill other human beings because people are nothing but illusions. This notion caused my world to wobble.

Illusions? I wondered. Other people? I can see other people. I can touch them. They are there. How can they be illusions? I thought of death. What about death? Is there anything left of people at death other than memories? If not, are we nothing but flickering flames that go up in smoke and disappear?

And I? An illusion? How can *I* be an illusion? Why then did Krishna's suggestion trouble me so? Was Arjuna looking at *me* as he listened to Krishna? Discovering that I was an illusion?

On that Halloween night I discovered that I was an illusion. Krishna's words bothered me precisely because I was coming to the same conclusions myself, although without such brutal clarity.

Weeks before Halloween, as I was walking to take the test for entry into law school, I had the sudden realization that I didn't want to be a lawyer. I *knew* this with certainty and I was filled with momentary joy. It was the least stressful exam I ever took. All my life I had thought I would be a lawyer. "Lawyer" was part of the structure of my being, of my future, of my vocabulary about myself. Of illusion.

Two years earlier I had stopped going to church. I remember the moment I made my decision. It was a Sunday afternoon. I was in the library with two friends. When I rose from the table, one of my friends asked where I was going. "To Mass," I answered. "Why?" he asked. When I realized that I didn't know, I sat down and began to study. No trauma, no crushing doubt, no lightning bolt from the sky. The end of an illusion.

Gradually, unknowingly, I had been discovering who I wasn't. I began writing poetry and stories in the months before Halloween, trying to come to grips with the bubblings and rumblings in my belly. "Poetry but it stinks/Yet it indicates that he thinks/About things to say/Before he goes away."

Into illusion? I would call my friends when one of my poems or little stories touched me. There was the story about the man who quit smoking and drinking. He took a trip to the Caribbean with the money he saved, only to die in a plane crash. Moral of story: it is hazardous to one's health to stop smoking.

"That's kind of weird," my friend said after I read it to him.

Here's another story. Two horses are trotting down the road. For no apparent reason, one horse jumps on the other's back, pushes him to the ground, and kicks him to death. A third horse is heard to mumble, "A classic case of horse's inhorsity to horse."

"I don't get that one at all, Andy," is the response I remember getting to that story.

Who can blame him? What can you expect from an illusion? Halloween. The time of ghosts and goblins. Of illusions seen and celebrated. Mocked in their illusory selves, as little ghosts and goblins travel the neighborhoods reminding us that if we but give them sweets, these horrifying creatures will go away for another year.

I never liked Halloween. Something in me believed in it more than I believed in Santa Claus. When other children entered the neighborhood House of Horrors on Halloween night giggling with joyful fear, I held back. I also hated Dracula movies. You could drive a stake through Dracula's heart, but he always came back to make another movie. And to haunt my dreams. Tell me, will you, what is the joy of pretending (I'm not convinced this is the right word) that vampires who want to suck your blood exist?

THE CRISIS

Halloween, though not traumatic, had been a yearly childhood festivity to be survived. I didn't survive Halloween in 1970 at age twenty-one. I discovered that I was an illusion.

Halloween morning I wrote in the back of the book I was reading (ironically, Herbert Marcuse's *One-Dimensional Man*) that "God is like the wind. You can see where He is by what He does." I liked the aphorism, but I didn't understand it.

The day proceeded normally (illusion) until dinnertime when I began to feel a pain in my chest. I called my good friend who was a premed student and told him of my symptom.

"Am I having a heart attack?" I asked.

"Do you have any pain in your left arm?" he asked me.

"Why?" was my nervous response.

"Because that would mean you are having a heart attack."

Instantly, my left arm started aching. I told him so.

"It's your mind playing tricks on you, Andy," he said firmly.

I repeated his words to myself. It's an illusion. You're not having a heart attack. You're not having a heart attack. You're not. I didn't.

After dinner, I went to a movie with my roommate. *Cat Ballou*, a silly comedy with Lee Marvin and Jane Fonda I think, not the stuff to produce an existential crisis. Not Bergman's *Seventh Seal*, not Fellini's *Satyricon*. You get my point. The existential problem entered the theater with me.

There is a scene in the movie that I don't remember clearly. All I remember is a noose. Lee Marvin's neck may have been in it. I don't know. I just remember the noose, and the feeling of death that swept over me. I wanted to shout, "Stop the movie! I'm dying!" But I didn't. Sanity, such as it was, leapt to my rescue. Or decorum. As though propriety were more important than life. Illusion.

I didn't cry out. I watched the rest of the movie. As I write this, it strikes me as incredible. Why aren't we crying out our desperation to each other? Why isn't the world full of bellows rather than silence? Why don't we hear each other's bellowing?

I didn't cry out. I talked to myself. I soothed myself with my earlier insight. You're not dying. You're a young man. You can't be dying. It's all in your mind. As though that could bring any comfort. Message: Relax, Andy, you're a wing ding. The world isn't changing at all. Don't worry, you're just going around the bend.

I left the movie. I didn't go have a beer with my roommate. Instead, I walked back to the dorm alone. Taking steps became more difficult. I feared that I would fall over; I would never make it back to my room alive.

I had to make it to my room. Why? Had to.

I entered the dorm. I didn't scream at the other students that I was dying. I stumbled to my floor where the walls were shimmering, breathing. I told myself, you're crazy, it's nothing. Trying to soothe myself. To convince myself that I was going to wake up from this.

It wasn't helping this time. The power to convince was gone. I went into the bathroom. My eyes caught the urinals, which looked like the stupidest things I had ever seen. The bathroom walls were breathing, too. I wondered then if someone had slipped me a drug. But I hadn't eaten anything. I hadn't drunk anything. Pharmaco-psychosis was not an out.

I opened my door. Went to the window. Looked ten stories down. I rushed to the phone and called my doctor friend. Not there. Desperately called another friend who couldn't come because he was working. But he found my other friend who rushed to see what was the matter. I cried out to him as he came in the door that I was dying. I was terrified. He put his arms around me and I wept for twenty minutes, or twenty years.

As the panic passed, my roommate returned, then another friend arrived. We talked about my options. It was clear to me, no doubts at all, that I was leaving school. My decision was whether to go to

Montana where I'd never been (something was calling me there) or to go home. My friends urged me to go home.

Next day, I drove thirteen hours home. Alone. Opportunities abounded to enter time warps. Space bent as my mind wandered. I smoked the pack of cigarettes that I'd bought for the trip. I hadn't smoked a cigarette in a year. I was hooked again. Instantly. Loved them because they behaved. You just light them, and breathe smoke in. Then blow smoke out. Smoke. Dependable. Cigarette smoke was my strongest certainty that something was real.

Finally I arrived home. I sat on the living room couch with my dad who shared his experience of uncontrollable shaking one night when he was a junior in college. A second piece of reality. Cigarette smoke and now a father who had been shaken by . . . something. It helped.

I stayed at home a week. Finally decided to return to school. Halloween wasn't about returning home. It was about facing my life. My death. Life.

Back at school, I attended classes. It didn't help. Nothing connected. Not even in Dunne's class. It was as though I had been eliminated from the game already. I sometimes woke up in the mornings with my chest aching and knew I was dying. Waking up just in time to experience it. But I didn't die. My body didn't. It limped to breakfast, to classes, through the day.

My friends and I talked, and talked, and talked. We agreed that we didn't understand what had happened and was happening to me. My doctor friend invited me to call him day or night if I needed to. He was a good doctor already. Even before med school. The next two weeks were full of middle-of-the-night terrors, phone calls, walks to his room, and night-long discussions.

But I wasn't getting better. And I was wearing down. A trip to the university counseling center proved very unsatisfactory. I felt misunderstood, patronized. I was getting more from my friends.

But they were wearing down, too. Worrying. Two of them were taking a premed course called Pain, Suffering, and Death, aimed at helping doctors-to-be see the human dimension of medicine. They presented my case to their professor who offered to see me if I wished.

THE RESCUE

I wished. I saw him the next week. I arrived at his apartment at six-thirty one evening. He and his wife had just finished dinner. I followed him upstairs to his study. Poured out my story again. Halloween. Chest pain. Movie. Walls. Dying. Home. Back. Desperation.

He stood, walked to me. Touched my arm. "I know what you're talking about," he told me. "The same thing happened to me twenty years ago."

What? Utter delight. The immediate sense that I wasn't totally alone in the universe. The craziness began to shift. Hope filled me. If a movie, this would be the moment for Beethoven's "Alleluia Chorus." Truly.

He reached for something, handed it to me. A crucifix.

"Hold onto this when you get panicked," he said. "It will help you."

I believed him! I, who two years earlier saw no reason to go to church. At a university full of crucifixes that hadn't touched me. This crucifix reached in and gave me hope.

I danced out of his office. *Danced.* Held onto that crucifix, like Dostoyevsky's character in *The Idiot* who greedily kisses a crucifix given him by a priest as he climbs the scaffold to die. I kissed the crucifix greedily as I walked *down* from the scaffold.

To live. This was the challenge before me. To find a way to live a life, *my* life. I met regularly with the professor. Daily the first couple weeks, then twice a week. I wrote a novel second semester telling the story of a young man who has an existential crisis. Who gets better. You get the picture. I was using story, images, to find my way.

THE HALLOWEEN MAN

Halloween was the beginning of new life for me, the end of an old life. Halloween has been my teacher ever since. I have learned more from Halloween about human beings than I ever did in graduate school. I, who hated Halloween, became the Halloween Man.

The Halloween Man. This is a new notion to me. I want to ponder it, to step into it. Halloween itself was the House of Horrors where I began to come alive. This is very strange. To feel at home in a House of Horrors. To find loving reality in the midst of existential despair and death.

What does that tell me about myself? About humanity? About you? We are death creatures, no denying that. All of us have loved ones who have gone to death, though for some, death holds no terror. They know that the universe is all right. They know that they go to God when they die. Or they comfortably accept that they go out of existence. This last type is shocking to me because I have a deep fear of going out of existence. And it makes life seem so stupid to me.

Years ago I had lunch with a dear friend who is a great lover of life and of people. As we talked, the subject of death arose.

"What do you think happens at death?" I asked her.

"Nothing, blessed nothing," she said.

"You don't want to go on?"

"It's the last thing I want," she said passionately. "I love life, Andy, but I have no need to live beyond this one."

I believed her. She was speaking true. Her words calmed me.

And yet, I have a tremendous need to live beyond this life. Halloween opens me to hollow places inside me, to urges to be and to become more, to become who I am meant to be, to mystery, to longings to connect to others, to other death creatures.

HALLOWEEN CONNECTIONS

I want to cry out to you: What do *you* think? What is life for you? What is waiting for you beyond life and in the middle of life? What do you know of Halloween?

You do know Halloween. Your Halloween will be shaped differently than mine, but you know it. You may run from it. You may deny it, but you know. You hear its whispers inside you. You remember experiences when life has let you down or torn you open. When life has been too much for you. A broken love affair. Loss of a job. Death of a parent, child, spouse. Rejection. Or that sense that everything isn't right within, or in the world.

You see a drunk careening down the street and for just a moment he is you. Or a cripple whose bent back causes her to walk slowly. Or a black man or a white woman or a Hispanic child, someone from whom you don't expect it, smiles at you. Something foreign inside you responds. You feel a moment's recognition. You feel something breaking open. You could, if you'd let yourself, run up to that person and hug him or her. At least you smile and a glow remains for awhile.

These are Halloween opportunities. Moments to hallow the hidden sprites and goblins, the mysteries of life which we usually deny ourselves. In this sense, Halloween is all around us. It is constantly happening and trying to be seen. Illusions are trying to become real before our eyes and in the middle of our hearts. Seeking to open us to greater life.

Why do we think that we understand life? Why do we think that our system of understanding is the truth, abiding and eternal? Why aren't we open to mysteries that daily befall us? Why do we not see surprise as opportunity rather than interruption?

Halloween teaches me. Walks beside me. Opens me to the mysteries that stand in front of me. Like yourself. Can you see yourself as a mystery? Can you stop for a moment and ponder the mystery of your life?

Realize that you are *here* even if you don't know where here is. Recognize that you have a life, that you are a life, a unique life, the likes of which won't be seen again after you're gone. Or won't be seen *here* anymore. Or won't be seen here unless you come back as someone else.

But you won't know who you were even then if you don't know who you are now. Do you? Do you know who you are? Are you all that you can be? Ask yourself that. Are you open to the possibility that you haven't even started to be who you are? Isn't that something to ponder? You aren't who you could be because you are too busy being who you aren't. Because that's who you think you are.

There is a Zen saying: "When walking, walk. When sitting, sit. Above all, don't wobble." But what if the world, your world, wobbles? What then? Can you wobble if there is an earthquake? Can you not?

I hope I haven't lost you. I hope I am pushing you to find yourself. I hope Halloween, in a gentle way, is opening to you. I hope you are wondering about yourself as much as you are about the guy who is writing this. I hope my strangeness invites yours rather than scaring you away.

THE POINT OF HALLOWEEN

I know that Halloween is scary. I even believe that that's its point. To scare us. But not away. To scare us open. To scare us toward each other. To get us illusions hugging each other, talking desperately about what matters to us, about the questions that fill our hearts. So that we can be real, so that we can shed the illusions that cloak us, hiding us from our true selves. So that we can become naked beings. Naked we enter this world and naked we should leave it.

I can't resist here mentioning Gary Larson's "Far Side" cartoon that shows all the contents of a house being sucked out a window into the sky. A woman is crying something like, "Oh God, Harold's taking it with him!"

What do we take with us? If you believe my friend, it's not a question because we're not going anywhere. A Beatles' song ends with the words, "The love you take is equal to the love you make." What do we take with us? Perhaps our naked beings. Perhaps we are here to begin to see our naked beings and to share them. Perhaps this makes our naked beings more real. Perhaps depression, whatever else it is, is the exhaustion we feel from covering up our naked beings.

We need to ponder why we cover ourselves up so, why we hide ourselves. Even if we think we know why. I am convinced that we are meant to share ourselves with others. I am convinced that we see our nakedness truly only as others do. When someone loves who you are, you are given the opportunity to love yourself more. But if you're so busy hiding, how in God's name can the other person see you and love you? So that you can see yourself and love yourself and become willing to show yourself more? So that the other person can see you and love you?

It's not as simple as that, is it? Often when you have shown yourself you have been hurt. We need to cloak ourselves, don't we? We need to discern to whom we can show our real selves. Our Halloween moments impel us to seek others. We live in dread that those others will reject us. Some of them will. Some of them won't be able to understand. Some of them will mock us. It can get very depressing.

Let's push on. Let's jump into what causes such isolation.

2

EVIL

For many years, I described Halloween as a time when evil crashed into my life and nearly destroyed me. Some force was bent on killing me. And it would have had I had not found the professor who shared the cross with me. Radical evil attacked me. Radical good saved me.

That is an understandable interpretation under such circumstances. Certainly, such dramatic experiences demand an explanation. Something in us seeks to bring order when chaos overwhelms us. It can be excruciating when order refuses to come. When the chaos hurts enough, we will look everywhere for order.

ENTERING UNKNOWN TERRITORY

Dante opens his *Divine Comedy* as a middle-aged man lost in a dark wood. He has come to an unknown, frightening, and painful place.

> Ay me! how hard to speak of it. That rude
> And rough and stubborn forest! The mere breath
> Of memory stirs the old fear in the blood;
> It is so bitter it goes nigh to death.

From that spot, he can see heaven in the distance, up a high mountain, and he longs to go there. He attempts to make the climb, to go straight to heaven, but is stopped on his way by three wild animals, a leopard, a lion, and a wolf. He cannot reach heaven directly. He must go by another way. Through hell.

We know what it is to come to an unknown place. We know the fear of such places. Perhaps great danger awaits us. Perhaps an adventure. We may not survive. We may find new life. If we step into the danger, we may be destroyed. If we walk away, we may miss the opportunity of a lifetime.

Ponder Dante's image. Find yourself alone in a dark wood. Feel the cool air. Listen to the sounds. The crunching pine needles under your feet. The peculiar bird calls. Stumble on the hidden rock beneath the needles and feel the pain in your twisted ankle shooting up your leg. Why did you separate from the others? Why did you tell them to go on their hike without you? Your face brushes against a branch unexpectedly. Your heart is beating faster. Now the dark of evening is beginning to fall. The cool air seems suddenly colder. A wild animal cries in the distance. Is it a hungry leopard, a lion, a wolf? You wonder about your friends. But there is nothing you can do for them, or expect from them now. Fear turns to terror in your belly. You must find another way if you are to survive. The animal cries again. You are alone.

Halloween. Suddenly you know that you are lost. You lose your job. You are diagnosed with a terminal illness. Your old landmarks are gone. You no longer can find your way because the familiar has become unfamiliar. It is hard to believe that you will ever find your way out of this dark place. That there even is a way out of here. The whole world has become dark. What are you to do? Is there any way to light up the world again, to return to the place you know?

An old song, by Skeeter Davis I think, is singing in my mind. The words go something like this. "Why does the sun go on shining? Why do the birds fly above? Don't say no. It's the end of the world. It ended when I lost your love." These are very typical lyrics, really. But it's the song that comes on my inner radio station. For the singer, the worst has happened. She has lost her love and the world has ended. Even though the sun shines, her world is darkness.

Anything can darken the whole world. Make it one great, big, dark wood. Send us into hell.

HELL

That's where Dante went. Is that where we're supposed to go when we're lost? That is potentially good news to people who are depressed and anxious. Profound depression *feels* like hell. It feels like lostness and darkness. The invitation to go to hell tells those lost in depression that they are on the right track.

But hell? *Hell?* That place in the middle of the earth where God sends bad people when they die? Many of us gave up the idea of hell years ago. It is a superstition. It is a way that our elders scared us into behaving. It is what scared *them* into behaving.

I remember an eighth grade experience that makes my point. A priest came into the boys' classroom to talk to us about sex. We had already been quarantined. Separated from the girls. Now we were going to get the word.

The priest told us the following story. A pretty girl was invited to a dance by a very handsome boy who had just moved to town. The night of the dance, just before he arrived to pick her up, she decided to wear a low-cut dress. At the last minute, just as the doorbell rang, she put her gold cross around her neck.

The party went wonderfully at first. He was charming, humorous, and a great dancer. She was the envy of all her girlfriends. Near the end of the party, he held her close, pressed himself against her, as the saxophone wailed seductively. She leaned her head back and tried to look into his eyes only to discover that he was instead staring down her dress. (As eighth graders, it didn't occur to most of us that it's just about impossible to press a woman close and look down her dress at the same time.) As she followed his eyes down to her breasts, she saw his feet. They had become hairy hooves! Seeing the gold cross between her breasts, an afterthought from God, he suddenly showed himself as the devil in disguise, then disappeared in a puff of smoke.

There's that smoke again. And another cross. Several teenage hearts were pounding that day at the end of the story. But it didn't stop most of us. Hell just didn't have the immediacy that our awakening sexuality did.

Is *this* the hell we don't believe in? Does disbelief in this hell disprove the existence of any hell? Remember the dark wood. Depression that feels like hell. To a depressed person it sometimes helps to have hell acknowledged. Not as punishment for being an evil human being, but as a reality experienced.

JOB

When we are depressed we know hell. We are in it. We aren't theologians trying to figure its size and shape, or whether it exists.

Our depression proves it. We, like Job, want to cry, "Why, why, why? Why am I here? Why are you doing this to me? My kids, my cattle, dead and gone. My body covered with boils. Why? What did I ever do to you, God, to upset you so?"

The beginning of the Book of Job presents God as somewhat naive. You know the story. God is feeling pretty good one day and is bragging to His heavenly court about Job. "He's such a righteous man. He's so faithful to Me. He's so good."

Satan, who is a member of the court, replies, "So what? You give him everything. Why shouldn't he be righteous? What's in it for him not to be? I tell you what, God. You zap the boy with a few troubles and you'll see his true colors."

God lets Satan zap Job and pretty soon God has an angry and confused creature asking for an audience. Job is scratching the sores he can reach and rubbing the hard-to-get-at places up against the dung heap as he cries out. You can imagine the crusted scabs on Job's face and chest. And his look of utter confusion because his world has fallen apart.

Job is doing something that we need to learn to do. He's banging at God's door. He's saying, "Look, the way I understand this thing, I've been doing pretty much what you want me to. Now you're doing to me what you promised you'd do to *bad* people. I know I must have broken some fundamental rule but which one? What did I do? Tell me. Tell me what I did. I'm not leaving until you do."

Job is crying out his honest anguish. He doesn't get it. Familiar, isn't it? A horrid turn of events in your own life makes you wonder the same thing. What did I do? Or else, now I'm getting it for something I did do. We can't seem to say, or to be satisfied anyway in saying, that's just the way it goes. Life is that way. You take the bitter with the sweet.

Let me change that. People *say* this to each other all the time. But we aren't thinking about what we're saying and we should stop. Because the message is so dreadful. "Your child is dead because bad things happen." "Your father died suddenly because God needed him somewhere else." A young woman told me people at her father's funeral said that to her. She was crushed.

No. It is all wrong. When tragedy happens, our souls are in anguish. We want to shout at our Job-friends who offer pious explanations, "Don't you dare explain my pain away! Don't you see that my loss is killing me?" But most of us have stifled our souls and instead cry into the great hollows inside ourselves.

Job cries at God. Do you get that? Job goes to God and yells for a hearing. How are we to cry out at God? What can make us dare? To look at Job is to think that daring is born of desperation. Of there being nothing left to lose.

THE STRUGGLE TO UNDERSTAND SUFFERING

We need to cry out to God, but most of us are a long way from doing so. It is too scary. Or we don't believe in God anymore. Or we have no energy because we are so depressed.

Return to Halloween with me again. Halloween showed me that I wasn't the strongest kid on the block. That the universe was more than I had fathomed before. That who I had been could cease to be with the snap of a cosmic finger, in the course of an evening.

As things started to improve for me, I was left with some difficult questions. Even if you survive an earthquake, you're left afterwards with several new holes in the road that you deny at your own risk.

I had to find some explanation for Halloween. Certain memories gave me a temporary solution. It had been awful. I hadn't done anything that I could remember to deserve it. It felt like something from beyond myself. I knew I wasn't capable of concocting or producing something so powerful. A cross had grounded me again. The explanation began to show itself. Something evil had gotten to me, the Devil if you will, and the cross freed me from it. It even sounded like good theology. Christ's victory over evil. In my own life.

This explanation sustained me for several years. It helped me hold together. It said that evil was real, but that it wasn't ultimate. I kept returning to Halloween, kept asking myself if I had it right. If it was that simple. But I could find no other satisfactory explanation, though I read dozens of books about evil. I read mythologies from around the world, from ancient times to the present. People have been struggling with evil for a long, long time, trying to find some explanation for it.

"Man, look no farther for the author of evil: You are he," Rousseau wrote in the eighteenth century. This is what Job's friends were telling Job, trying desperately to convince him that *he* must have done something terribly wrong. Because if he hasn't, *their* world falls apart. The same things could happen to them. Better that he carry the burden than that they be challenged to see a new possibility.

I'm not knocking this belief. It helped me survive. It helped me become solid. It gave me a sense of how evil can be involved in a person's life, in my life. But it didn't answer all my questions. I began to understand that we can't just answer the question of evil. Rather, we have to live with the reality of it. We have to confront it, contend with it, cry out to the forces of good to prevail.

I held on to this view for many years though I continued to question it. Something about it troubled me. I had a hard time sharing it with others. It embarrassed me to say my life was changed by an encounter with evil and by the victory of good over evil. I couldn't admit what had happened except when I felt very safe. It made me feel too odd.

In 1982, I decided I wanted to write a book on the humanity of Jesus. I wanted to get at the person, to present Jesus as a vibrant being, fully human, whose very humanity showed us how to get to God. But I was having trouble with the book. The material was there, but it lacked fire. I hadn't put myself into it. After much inner struggle (and rejections by publishers), I realized that I needed to tell the reader what had brought me to write a book about Jesus.

This took me back to Halloween. To the cross. How could I explain what had happened to me? I had encountered a deep humanity with that cross. And what went before the cross? Halloween. I held my breath, wrote furiously, and explained it as evil. I had been saved from evil.

Why would a man who has been saved feel embarrassed by it? What if I had instead been pulled from freezing waters? Would I have felt embarrassed? If I'd done something stupid to get me there, maybe. It becomes clear that there's a problem here. Probably many problems. Intellectually, I couldn't decide what had happened to me. Not *that* it happened, but what it meant. It made me feel peculiar. And isolated.

Now we're getting closer. I feared telling my story because in telling it, I could be rejected. Could be seen as crazy. Halloween. In attempting to protect myself from feeling isolated, I was isolating myself. There is something ominous here. The reality of evil. Isolating myself in the act of protecting myself from isolation.

I screwed up my courage. Wrote a preface that told my Halloween story, opened to the reader why this human being Jesus was so important to me. I said there what I've already said here. That I was overcome by evil and found my way back through the cross.

My heart is beating fast as I write. I'm in new territory right now. I can feel an insight coming to me. I don't quite see it yet. Maybe it has to do with the pervasiveness of isolation in life, the death-bringing quality of it, the awesome power of it. And the fact that I'm still here, telling my story, pondering it, opening to new mysteries. Another proof—I hope my words can convey it—that something awesomely good *is*. Is in the world. Is seeking us.

HOW IS GOD INVOLVED IN OUR SUFFERING?

Understanding the Human Jesus was published with the above mentioned preface in early 1985. Two weeks after publication of the book, I led a workshop in Washington, D.C. at which most of the participants had read the book. Several comments were made at the conference. The most upsetting of them (said by more than one person) was "I don't think your Halloween experience was evil. I think it came from God."

God? God! The comment gave my world another wobble. My reply? "No, it was evil."

"God can bring discomfort," one of them said.

"You aren't listening to me. I know it was evil." You can almost feel the cement hardening in my attitude.

"What about St. Paul? It couldn't have felt good to hear a voice challenging him. Or to get knocked off his horse. Or to go blind."

"I'm not St. Paul."

On and on they went, telling me that religious experiences happen to all kinds of people. Many of whom aren't the ones seen as traditionally good or holy.

To shut them up I humored them. "Okay, I hear what you're saying. I'll think about it." Meanwhile, I was thinking, "The book's just two weeks old, for God's sake. The ink isn't even dry. These people aren't letting me say what it has taken me such a long time to find the courage to say."

They jarred me. They were trying to help me. Wouldn't it be good news if God, not evil, came to me that Halloween?

Even now, there is a part of me who wants to shout back at them,

"If you can say that, you don't know what in hell you're talking about."

Let's let this be complicated. In some profound sense, I think they were right and we'll get to that. God was in on it. But the isolation and terror were overwhelming. God? Then it is indeed a fearful thing to fall into the hands of the living God. I feel no great love for this living God at this moment. I want to shout, with Job next to me scratching his sores, "What the hell do you think you're doing, God? Can't you find some other way to reach me? Lover, hah!"

The deeply cynical one in me appears. Another insight comes. Here it is. I don't want to let God come out of this looking like the chivalrous knight.

For the timid reader who thinks this is no way to speak to God, the house hasn't fallen on me yet. Sometimes this is the only way to talk to God. When people's souls are at stake, we must cry out whatever helps them. Even give them a cross they don't believe in. Or a hug. Or a Buddhist prayer wheel. Or cry with them. At least that. Give them some impossible hope in the midst of their hopelessness. Maybe, maybe we will touch them and break their damnable isolation. In W. H. Auden's words: "Nothing can save us that is possible/We who must die demand a miracle."

A woman in dire straits moaned these words to me: "I need to pray and I don't know how." I asked her, "What would you say to God if you could say anything?" Her immediate response was, "Goddammit, God, you've got to help me." This is true prayer. She began to feel connected to God almost instantly because she was being real. Any God that can't accept reality, that isn't up to human anguish, is pathetic. Walker Percy instructs: "Attack the false in the name of the real." Yes. And again: "Beware of people who think everything is okay."

Everything isn't okay. Halloween. Dark wood. Starvation. Nuclear weapons. Cancer. Depression and anxiety. Isolation. You can almost feel the heartbeat of the negative, can almost feel it thrumming, drawing at you, pulling, seducing you toward loneliness, away from others.

What about you? In what ways are you isolated? How do my words make you feel? Do they resonate within you? Anger you? Is it clear to you that I'm a lost soul who doesn't know what he's talking about? Or a searching soul who is finding some ways to move ahead? Who is met by God right in the middle of the mess of himself? Thrown to the mat. Pinned. One, two, three. God, again, is the winner. But what? A picture comes to me of God weeping over the broken mess lying there.

RANDOMNESS

Evil messes up the universe. It messes up philosophical systems. We can try to be tidy by taking the blame ourselves, saying with Rousseau and Job's friends that it's all our fault. This feels fine and dandy, until we find ourselves in a pickle, until the world turns against *us* and we are the ones left weeping and wailing and gnashing our teeth.

I have in front of me an article by Jenilu Schoolman which challenges what I have just written. Schoolman is a psychologist who discovered several years ago that she had liver cancer. She writes in this article about her experiences with the illness and its remission. During chemotherapy, as she lost her hair, images of concentration camp victims with their shaved heads comforted her. They showed her that she was not alone in dying young or unfairly. She was "but a mere victim of the randomness of the universe . . . Someone has to die of cancer, why not me?"

Randomness gave Schoolman courage. It told her that she wasn't being punished for some unknown sin. She took comfort that she was not alone, that horrible injustice has happened to others, too. Randomness freed her. For me, randomness as the ultimate principle of the universe causes despair. I think that neither one of us is wrong. I wouldn't try to take away from her the gift of the universe's randomness. Nor, I suspect, would she push me toward the terror into which ultimate randomness brings me. Ponder for a moment that randomness can free one person and destroy another. This is very strange. To paraphrase J. B. S. Haldane: Reality may not only be stranger than we imagine. It may be stranger than we *can* imagine.

In a sense, I know randomness. On Halloween I was confronted by it. I experienced the horror of feeling disconnected from everything. I was a random piece of protoplasm in a random universe. About to die. I couldn't stand it, or stand up under it. It crushed me.

Randomness opened me to the emptiness of my soul. When I stopped going to church, I experienced the emptiness of my position as freeing. I was casting off what was, for me, a dead system. The relief of not carrying around all that dead weight was momentarily delightful. But gradually the emptiness took on a life of its own. It became more than the mere absence of dead belief, more than freedom. It became itself, a palpable emptiness that confronted me. I was forced to see that *I* was empty, that nothing was propelling me forward. I became my own dead weight. It was time for me to die.

RENAMING

Leap to 1985. To Washington, D.C. To the idea that God brought about my Halloween experience. What could that mean? That God wasn't who I thought? That the crucifix had some different meaning than the one I had named? Could the cross save me from *God*? That line of thinking didn't help me. And yet, what if God *was* calling me to be? What if God was calling me to live in a new, more vital, truer way? That was exciting to me.

But I still sensed that something evil was involved in my Halloween experience. I remember a dream that a woman once told me in which she looked into her dining room and saw someone whom she was convinced was evil. Later in the dream, she saw this person again and realized that he was not evil at all. He was holy. The dream challenged her to rename an aspect of her life that she had seen as evil. I was struggling with the same problem. Was Halloween an invitation from God? Or was I falling for someone else's explanation? And what about that sense of the presence of evil?

There was no simple solution. Gradually, a creative compromise unfolded in me. I accepted the possibility that God *could* have been the one who brought on my terrifying experience. In that case, God was calling me from death into new life.

To my thinking, it was a very loud call, leading me to suspect that I had grown quite deaf. And that I was also quite dead. What do I mean when I say I was dead? I was a senior in college, I had friends, had a girlfriend back home. I was doing well in school, making good grades. But *I* was dead. The "I" in me, the "me" of me was dead. To paraphrase Mark Twain: "The rumors of my living were greatly exaggerated."

Okay. Dead. But evil? Where is this evil I have been harping about? Right there in the middle of my apparent life. In my dead life. In the emptiness that had replaced my old beliefs. Evil was the force of death, of self-denial, that had cut me off from my essence. I was not living *my* life. Recall the joy I felt when I realized that I didn't want to be a lawyer. That was my life calling out to me. But I didn't hear it. I heard only a negation of a negation.

God came noisily on Halloween. I had missed the less painful invitations. Because I was so dead. Because my true being was so isolated that I didn't know who I was.

Evil is isolation. We serve evil whenever we serve isolation. I'm not talking about taking needed time to be by yourself. Or about saying no to another person because you have nothing to offer. In fact, as I will argue in the rest of this book, one of the main avenues of true escape from isolation is to go into hell, into the depths of our inner beings, into our depression, to confront that which isolates us, and to find that which calls us into relationship with other people and with God.

I want to leap ahead for just a moment. To say to you that ultimately you don't have to be isolated. To tell you that there are outer and inner beings who want to help you. To say what I believe to be the fundamental truth of life. That the core of life is relational. The core of life calls to us even in our isolation. There are ways to open to that core. The first way for some of us is to step, like Dante, into our own hellish suffering.

3

ISOLATION

The English word *isolate* is related to the Italian *isola*, meaning "separated as an island," and derives from Latin *solus*, "alone, solitary." There is a possible connection between *solus* and the Greek *holos*, meaning "whole, entire." From *solus* we get the English words *solitude*, *solitary*, and *soliloquy*, the last word from Latin *soliloquium* meaning "an alone speaking."

John Donne, the British Protestant divine and poet, wrote "No man is an island, entire of itself; every man is a piece of the continent, a part of the main." Isolation makes islands of us, complete but incomplete. Separated from the rest of the world. Out of communication. Some islands are paradises, like Tahiti. But others are hell, like Devil's Island. Perhaps inhabitants of Tahiti-like islands would just as soon be left alone. But inhabitants of Devil's Island are captives, caught in the swamps, unable to find their way to freedom.

STEPPING INTO ISOLATION

As we begin our journey into isolation, let's remember what Dante knew, that the way to heaven is through hell, that the way to connection is through opening to all that isolates us. Do you see the great possibilities carried in the word itself? If we can explore our isolation, we may find solitude, the place from which are born great discoveries. We may find that our solitude is related to wholeness. Or even, as Dante found, that the goal and reward of the journey into isolation is the Celestial White Rose, is God.

Such thoughts and hopes enable us to step onto Devil's Island. Notice how your hope begins to fade as you plod through the steamy, alligator-filled swamps of your soul. Your clothes stick to your skin as mosquitos buzz and bite mercilessly. It is a harsh place, your soul, Devil's Island.

What a starting point for a journey! And what a motivation to move if you can escape it. Devil's Island. Devil's isolation. Alone with the Devil. Such is the place of depression and hopelessness. And those bugs! (Bug, as colloquial for insect, means "a creepy-crawly form of life," and derives from the basic sense of "goblin." Ah, so it's Halloween on Devil's Island.) Those damn bugs are whispering, buzzing in our ears. The Devil's soliloquy.

There is an alone speaking, a *soliloquium*. An alone full of negativity which speaks in you. You know its words. You have thought them often yourself: "I am no good. I am a failure. I can do nothing right. Better that I'd never been born."

Those words are bugs that buzz and bite. The voice continues in you. Let's call it the Voice of Aloneness. "It's hopeless. There is no way out."

So you plod through the muddy swamp of yourself, bitten by such inner words. How can you possibly escape Devil's Island when the Devil uses your very own voice to keep you there? You are accepting these negative words as fact. Aren't you? Don't you believe these words whispering inside you?

It just isn't true that you're no good. You're not a total failure. No matter what you've done in your life. Even if you have done something truly terrible. Even if you've murdered someone.

And yet, it isn't always the things called evil by the world that defeat us. Years ago I worked with a woman who lived a life full of affairs, divorce, and broken friendships. Though these things bothered her, her deepest secret was surprising. She walked into my office one day and spoke before she sat down. "Andy, I've discovered something terrible about myself," she said anxiously. "When I tell you, you will probably ask me to leave your office."

"What is it?" I asked her, aware that she was about to share her most horrible secret with me.

"I'm petty," she whispered and burst into tears.

The other problems in her life had bugged her, were noises buzzing around her head. But when the Voice of Aloneness spoke, it said, "I'm petty. I'm small. I'm picky and critical. I focus on the imperfection of others and not their goodness. I am an awful person."

We mustn't try to talk a person out of such a discovery. Or use reason to attempt to explain it away. Though this is exactly what we often do. We say, "There, there. Pettiness isn't such a big thing. You're a good person. Snap out of it." But if we say this, we push the person even further into isolation. We are giving the message, "Your biggest concern is unimportant." And with this, *we* become the mosquitos that are buzzing around her head.

Another woman taught me about the destructiveness of little lies. "If something cost me 39 cents, I'd say it cost 29 cents. If I could buy something and hide it from my husband, I would. But the lies became my life, my definition of myself." Gradually, the cumulative weight of her little lies was crushing her. To say to her, "For goodness sakes! You just took ten cents off the price. That doesn't matter" is to miss the profoundly isolated person who is sinking further and deeper into the swamp, caught in the eternal soliloquy of the Voice of Aloneness saying, "I am a liar. I am a liar."

What can we do when we discover someone in this kind of situation? First, we need to enter that person's isolation. We have a word for this: consolation. To be alone *with*. To listen with the isolated one to that Voice of Aloneness. To respond in some different way than Job's friends did.

But we must never say to a person caught in grief and isolation, "You *are* petty. You *are* a liar." Rather, we can say "Something in you is calling you petty. Something is calling you a liar."

But what if the person *is* petty, *is* a liar? Then her recognition and sharing of this is cause for rejoicing. We are being invited to share the truth of her isolation. Do you see what profound admissions these two women made? And what a gift they gave to me? Each handed me her desperate secret. Gave me what was isolating her from humanity. Named the mechanism of her despair.

THE VOICE OF ALONENESS

I say to people who have made such an admission, "Let the charges stay but imagine someone else making them against you. Thus it is an other, an accuser, who says, '*You* are petty. *You* are a liar.' Listen to your accuser."

With this, something often shifts for the person. A differentiation has begun. The Voice of Aloneness is now an other. An inner being speaking in one's soul. As other, it can be challenged.

You might try this yourself right now. Open to those negative charges you regularly make against yourself, like, "I'm no good, I'm selfish, I betray my friends." Hear those charges and see your predicament. You are locked in an argument with yourself. But if there is an *other* speaking these words? The feeling shifts, doesn't it, when you hear the words, "You are no good, selfish, a betrayer"? You have taken an extremely important step when you make this shift. You have heard the Voice of Aloneness speaking as other.

But this is Devil's Island. This other has bullwhips and manacles. Can throw you deeper into isolation.

Yes. And this is exactly what has been happening all along. And it is hell's way, a picture of the inferno. Through places like this Dante trudged with Virgil. Through places like this must we pass to get to heaven.

Then do we even want to get to heaven?

That's a good question. I do. I bet you do, too. You want out of this hellish place. And maybe you now see a faint glimmer of hope.

But this aloneness, imaged and seen, can be frightful. Many people have shared with me images that match in power images of old of devils with pitchforks, of gorgons with hair of snakes, of devouring, raging monsters. One said, "It is like there is a great open mouth that will crush me with its teeth." Another said, in pictures reminiscent of Kafka, "A prosecutor points his steely finger at me. I feel condemned." Still another added, "A gigantic vehicle rolls toward me. It will grab me in its shovel and crush me." Madeleine L'Engle in her book, *A Wind In The Door*, pictures this aloneness as the *echthroi*, which are shrieking expressions of the force that would "nothing" us, that would write us completely out of existence.

Hell is not some place in another world. It is inside us. We know it. We hear it speaking. In times of depression and despair, we rail against ourselves. "I'm petty. I'm a liar. I'm no good." That is the isolation of the Voice of Aloneness. A Voice that accuses. An adversary. Which is what *satan* means. A satan is an adversary, an accuser. One who would bring us to nothing. But hear Mephistopheles, the devil in Goethe's *Faust*, say of himself that he is "part of that force which would do evil, yet forever works the good."

These words of Mephistopheles may induce hope in us. But it is hope in the wrong thing. For they invite us to naïveté. Evil brings no automatic shift from hell to heaven. Simply stated, evil *noth-ings*; it opens our souls to Devil's Island. *Confronting* evil is what works for good. *Hearing* the Voice of Aloneness as an accuser, as an adversary, works for good. Finding out what that satan holds in isolation works for good. *Toward* good. Takes us one more step through hell toward our goal.

But it doesn't transport us magically to a land of bliss. Heaven isn't a land of bliss. I believe that heaven is related reality. Whatever we leave behind of ourselves in hell, leave isolated there, will drag us back to Devil's Island. There is no escaping isolation except by moving through it—in relationship.

BEGINNING TO SHARE ISOLATION

I remember a woman crying out to me as she began to come out of her depression, "I am a lonely star in the distant heavens. You are the only other star I see and you are light years away from me." I answered her; "At least now, you aren't the only star visible in the night sky." She agreed. The *totality* of her isolation had ended.

I remember a man who had been a member of a cult. It chilled my soul when he said to me, "[The leader of the cult] has moved inside me. He has pushed Jesus outside of me and turned my heart black." It grieved me when I heard later that he had committed suicide. Isolation had swallowed him up.

Isolation can kill. It can keep us from developing. Children who are held and cuddled are not only happier than those who are not held, they also grow better and are healthier. They *thrive*. So Rene Spitz demonstrated in a foundling home half a century ago. And yet, we knowingly and unknowingly isolate ourselves from each other. Just like Spitz's little orphans, *we* fail to thrive when we are not held, cuddled, listened to, and loved.

Let me give you an example. A man sat across from me with his fists clenched, giving voice to his greatest pain. "I don't understand how I could *choose* nothing!" he all but yelled at me. We had been talking about his lifelong tendency to avoid connection with others, including his wife and children. As we explored his past experiences, we gradually understood that he had seen only one option open to him from early childhood. If he tried anything as a child, if he attempted to become an individual in any way, his parents had made him feel that he was bad. He saw no good in himself. There was only badness. Every step toward being himself had been squashed. But there was a profound longing in him to be good, to discover the good he somehow knew was there. He imaged this goodness as a bag of gold that he sometimes could grab in his hands. On the rare occasions when he succeeded in taking hold of the gold, he rejoiced and knew the goodness that was in him.

But only for that moment. As soon as he let go of the gold it ceased to exist for him. "How could I choose nothing?" he pressed me. I tried to answer him, but he only got more agitated. He hit his leg with his fist. "This is crucial, Andy. I cannot *choose* nothing. People don't choose *nothing*. I need an image to help me understand. I have no image for nothing."

His wife, who was sitting with us, leaned forward and said, "Honey, you don't choose nothing. You choose not to be bad. When you see no other options, you fall back into the nothing, into nonexistence, and keep waiting for another opportunity to be."

I added, "The nothing is the uncreated place (as he and I had observed many times before) where you are caught in your nonexistence. Every specific act you do is a step out of the nothing, is your person daring to be."

The effect of this interchange was striking. He was suddenly, tangibly, more present. His expression evidenced that we had heard him. It was like watching someone awaken to a new world. His wife and I had just observed *him* in the nothing. We had heard the Voice of Aloneness speaking in him and seen how it engulfed him in blackness and nothingness. Only by entering his isolation with him could we touch him so deeply. As he told us, he had not been touched this way before. To deny his experience of nothingness was to deny his very life. Which is exactly what had been happening since he was a little child. Paradoxically, we can't bear having our isolation denied. Because *that* isolates us even more. We need someone to enter our isolation with us.

This is one of the truly daunting things about relationship. All of us (or so I believe) have places of nothingness inside us, parts of ourselves that we have banished, that long to come alive in us. When we stumble upon them, our usual response is to shove them back into the nothingness. To banish our isolated selves. Who are we serving when we do this? The one who runs Devil's Island? Do we become in some sense "part of that force which would do *good,* yet forever works the evil?"

BANISHING THE ISOLATED ONE

Banishment is a harsh reality. In traditional cultures, a person who breaks a taboo may be banished from the tribe, cast out forever, and considered dead. Such a person may also die in fact. Just drop over dead from isolation, from being disconnected from the community.

When we isolate some part of ourselves, does *it* die? Do we lose it forever when we banish it? Yes. Unless we will go into the wilds of ourselves, into the dark wood, into hell's isolation to find it.

I work with many people who feel banished from their families and from the world around them. They try many things to hide from the pain of banishment. It is not uncommon for them to over-eat. They try to fill themselves with food when what they long for is connection to others.

Overeaters Anonymous calls overeating the disease of isolation. A young woman who had just become abstinent a week earlier said to me, "I know now that overeating is a disease. When I am over-eating, I am isolating myself, making myself unreachable, when what I long for more than anything is to be reached." She came to see that overeating masked her real feelings so that she wasn't free to be her natural self with others. This, in turn, distanced others from her, which led her to feel more isolated. And then to more over-eating. Then to embarrassment because of weight gain. Then to turning down invitations to be with others because she didn't want them to see her. Which brought on still more isolation. So that her isolation deepened and fed on itself. The food that was to nour-ish her lonely self had instead pushed her more deeply into her loneliness.

Another woman with an eating disorder told me the following dream she had as she began to experience her deep issues. "I am flying to Hungary with an unknown woman friend for holiday. My mother has paid for our hotel room in Budapest." She laughed as she considered the pun—the state of "Hungry." She was traveling to this hungry land in a new way, with a new friend, an as yet unknown part of herself. She was not alone. Her mother, whose own inner problems had helped prevent this woman from taking a conscious journey to her hungry place, was now cooperating and contributing to her exploration. Where before there was only despair, now she felt the hope of healing, *if* she would travel to the heart of her hunger. To her Devil's Island.

As I tell these stories, I again fill with the awareness of how much isolation there is in the world. How much hidden aching. How many secrets that are never told. That are left sitting before the altar of the Voice of Aloneness, as sacrifices to the negative, and as instruments that can be used to serve it.

And you? What about your places of isolation? Your hidden secrets? Does the mention of them cause you to squirm? Do you want to run away from me? Or perhaps pour them out finally to another human being? Do you feel the heaviness of your isolation? Do you have a sense of the Voice of Aloneness in you? Are you up against it all by yourself? If you are, it isn't a fair fight. You don't have a chance. The Voice of Aloneness knows all about you. Knows those things you won't dare share with another. Uses the fact that you can't share them to beat on you.

The Voice speaks, doesn't it? It says something like, "So, you've done something that you're too ashamed to tell anyone, haven't you? I am your only company here. I know who you are and what you are. If others knew they would banish you. What further proof do you need that you are life unworthy of life, as the Nazis said of the Jews?"

These are powerful words. And convincing. You are trapped with the Voice of Aloneness. In your inner hell. Does it hurt enough to cry out your pain to another? Do you want to shout at me, "I have many times tried to cry out my pain and been rejected. I can't risk it again?" Do you accept the banishment of this part of yourself? If you do accept banishment, you are looking at one of the reasons for your depression.

RELATING IN ISOLATION

It has been hard for me to write these chapters. To step again into my negativity and isolation. Because, as you no doubt see clearly, I am vulnerable to it. To speak of it casts me into it. To share isolation opens my isolation. In a way, that is terrible. But how else could it be? To talk about isolation in the abstract is to leave *you* in isolation.

I must warn you that we don't leave isolation for good when we deal with it once. I recognize a valuable pun in my words "leaving isolation for good." Maybe we do leave isolation for good. It's just that we don't leave it permanently. Why is this so? Experience tells me that there are at least two reasons.

First, there are so many areas of isolation in each of us, some so removed from us, so cut off, that we don't even know they exist. Only as we share with other isolated people and open to them are we opened to these hidden, painful places in ourselves. Which is to say that relationship opens us to isolation.

What's going on here? Relationship *does* open us to isolation. It brings us to the Voice of Aloneness speaking inside us and exposes that hidden dialogue to the world beyond ourselves, by showing it to another human being. By so doing, relationship brings isolation to relationship. Are you with me? Relationship permits isolation to become part of the world without killing the isolation, without banishing it or you.

Second, the isolation of others calls out to us, awakens us to their aches. Something in us hates isolation so much that (here we go again) we want to banish it, to free our friends from it. To cast it into hell. But that doesn't work. Because isolation is magnetic. It is an emptiness drawing us toward it. Worse than this, our isolation often contains just what we need to go forward in our lives. I sometimes yell at God, "Why do you have to hide all this good stuff *here*? Why not some more comfortable place?"

There is a great mystery encircling, longing to emerge from, isolation. There is Another Alone speaking inside us. Or better, moaning inside us. Trying to get our attention. Another Alone does not serve isolation. Rather, it goes to the heart of isolation precisely because that is where we are lost. I believe that Another Alone loves us, that it endures the aloneness, moaning and crying, in the hope that we will hear that we are not lost even where we *are* lost. That we are not damned in our damnation. That truly and honestly opening to hell exposes something greater than hell. Which is why (besides having no choice) we are journeying through hell together now.

TWO BROKEN HEALERS

In Buddhism, the *bodhisattva* is an enlightened being who has transcended the cycle of death and rebirth, and who *chooses* to stay on the wheel of life and death in order to help other beings find enlightenment. I want to propose the image of the *broken* bodhisattva, which I define here as one who has been freed from painful isolation enough to be willing to re-enter it with another. I have known several broken bodhisattvas in my life. Curiously, it is their brokenness that has most moved me, not their enlightenment.

Several years ago a man with a terminal illness was referred to me. He was quite dissatisfied with his life and had attempted suicide. As we talked I discovered that he believed in reincarnation and that he felt his present life was a bust, a failure. If he could die, maybe his next life would be more fulfilling. I considered him to be at risk of suicide because he evidenced no fear of death.

I asked him early in our conversations if he was concerned about carrying over to his next life the unresolved issues of his present life. He supposed that he was, but in another life he might have a better chance to resolve these issues. I saw more clearly that he was an isolated man who had hidden the truth of himself from his friends and family.

I asked him if he would be willing to try to resolve some of his concerns before he died. He said he might be. But he wasn't enthusiastic. I then took a risk. I told him that his lack of fear of death intrigued me. Unlike himself, I had no such comfort with death. Perhaps he could teach me his lack of fear.

With that we stepped into his isolation and into my fear. Point-counterpoint. "I feel like giving up and dying," he said. "I'm scared to death of dying," I said. He didn't tell me how to overcome my fear of death. He showed me. I didn't tell him how to come out of his isolation. I joined him there.

Gradually, as his health slowly deteriorated, his spirit came alive. He began to open to his family and his friends. To let them see who he really was. And to his great surprise, rather than rejecting him, his friends embraced him, and his family asked his forgiveness for all the hurt they had unknowingly caused him.

The time came for him to die. He still wasn't afraid. He was even more eager to go. But now there was more inside him than the Voice of Aloneness that had told him to end his life. Now he was

dreaming at night of going to sporting goods stores to buy equip-
ment for his upcoming journey. And I was a little less frightened of
death.

DARING TO HOPE

Isolation is such a hard place for hope to reside. But hope sometimes
hangs out in harsh places. Listen to the words of Vaclav Havel,
Czech playwright, dissident, and now president of his country.
Hope, he says, is

> an ability to work for something because it is good, not just because it
> stands a chance to succeed. The more unpropitious the situation in
> which we demonstrate hope, the deeper that hope is. Hope is definitely
> not the same thing as optimism. It is not the conviction that something
> will turn out well, but the certainty that something makes sense,
> regardless of how it turns out. In short, I think that the deepest and
> most important form of hope, the only one that can keep us above
> water and urge us to good works, and the only true source of the
> breathtaking dimension of the human spirit and its efforts, is some-
> thing we get, as it were, from 'elsewhere.' It is also this hope, above all,
> which gives us the strength to live and continually to try new things,
> even in conditions that seem as hopeless as ours do, here and now.
> (Vaclav Havel, *Disturbing the Peace*)

Sharing another's isolation is an act of desperate hope. It says
"No!" to the isolating Voice of Aloneness. It dares to believe that
what it needs to be is so. That there is Another Alone crying out
to us, from the depths of our isolation, using our discomfort and
depression to reach us. Is this possible? Is our isolation not ultimate? Is the Ultimate most present where we feel most alone?

4

REALITY

We have stepped into hell. We have admitted our isolation. We have confronted the Voice of Aloneness that seeks to confine us and push us even further into the hell of isolation. We have sensed Another Alone who wants to meet us right in the middle of that same isolation. It shouldn't surprise us if questions about the very nature of reality begin to press at us. In fact, how could it be otherwise?

ADMITTING THE REALITY OF HELL

Here are some of the scary and aching questions that come to me when I listen to the Voice of Aloneness. Is hell the ultimate reality? Is each one of us finally alone, isolated, unable to share our deepest beings? Is this journey an exercise in futility that can only end in nothingness, no matter how much we desire it to be otherwise? If so, shouldn't we just drop to the ground right here and give up? Or search out the least painful resting place we can find and wait for our end? An end that proves to us that life itself is an *echthros*, which ultimately nothings us by wiping us out of existence.

How do you respond to this picture of ultimate reality? How do you feel about it? Does it open in you a deepening dread? Does it increase your anxiety? Or comfort you that at least this nonsense will one day end? Does this picture *deepen* your depression? Do you hear the Voice of Aloneness speaking, asking similar questions in you? If I practice what we have already learned and let the Voice speak to me as an other, these are the words I hear. This is how I imagine the Voice responding to these questions: "You *are* alone, friend. In the end, I'm all you've got. And even I am not real.

Everything ends. Love ends. Friendship ends. Life ends. Finally, everything will be gone, even I. All you will have left is your awakened self, isolated in an unending nothingness."

Am I upsetting you as I let the Voice of Aloneness speak? Or are you at peace with going out of existence? It could be the latter, though I doubt a person with that view would be making this journey with me. For such a journey would seem utter stupidity. "I should waste my time worrying about hell when this life is all I've got? Hah!"

But some of us have no choice but to "waste our time here." Because this is where we find ourselves. Just as some people find themselves in the Black Hole of Calcutta. Hell itself is insistent. Is our present reality. It won't let us flee into denial of it. Instead, it takes the denial and turns that into hell. Do you see? Hell is such a perverse reality that even the denial of it brings us further into it.

Feel what it is like for you when you deny hell. When you refuse to be in the middle of your isolation but have no way to escape it. Feel how depressing it is not to admit where you are to another person. Or who you are. When you do this, when you deny your reality, you become, as the Voice of Aloneness says, like a nothing, denying a nothing, but with no ability to escape it. The nothing itself grabs you.

If you ask me, this is very creepy. To be in the land of the nothing where nothing tortures us by being nothing. It doesn't make sense, does it? How can a nothing be so powerfully upsetting? The philosopher Leibniz wrote, "Quod non agit non existit." "What does not act does not exist." If the nothing doesn't act, it doesn't exist. That's simple enough. But if it acts? Then perhaps we have misnamed it. It is something, not nothing. Or we've got all sorts of problems if nothings can disturb us so much. Reminds me of Halloween again. With goblins bugging us and nothings terrorizing us.

WHAT IS YOUR REALITY?

An image of a farmer comes into my mind. I see him scratching his head as he stares at me. All my musing must seem to him like craziness. Why does this image come now? A farmer farms. He doesn't spend his time wondering if something is real. Or if nothing is something. To him, all this is foolishness. He plows his field, plants, harvests, then sells his crops. All very practical. Maybe he comes to remind me of the solid ground that can bring forth life and food. I am grateful for the reminder, but I cry out to him in return that hell is real, too. That this so-called nothing you and I are exploring is some kind of something.

But what possesses us to call it nothing? It brings depression. It stops us in our tracks. It acts. Why would we even consider something that can do all that a nothing? It's so strange, isn't it? The first hint that there was something in the middle of our depression was the Voice of Aloneness speaking. But the Voice serves the nothing, serves that which brings everything to nothing. Doesn't it? With its "You're no good, you're a liar, it's hopeless" talk.

I think it's time for us to stop for a minute. To regroup. To see where we are. For starters, let's acknowledge that we have stepped into the reality of the hell of depression. We are marching through this hell together. Trying to deal with isolation, to open it, to bring it along with us. So we can get to that other place, up that mountain that we couldn't climb before. The Voice of Aloneness has been speaking to us. For just a moment, Another Alone was a real possibility. And now the nothing has crept in again. And with it our depression with its boring refrain of "Isolation, nothingness, hopelessness. Isolation, nothingness, hopelessness." How did that happen? What sleight of hand took hell away from us? And us with it?

Reality did. What do I mean? How did reality dissolve hope? By telling us that only hell is real, or that there is no hell. By telling us that this journey is ridiculous, that God doesn't moan in the middle of our isolation. We lose our ability to fight isolation and nothingness when this happens. And if we stay focused on this, we will fall deeper into depression.

Am I right? Does this talk eat at your hopefulness? Are images of hope slipping away? Do you see the power our view of the world has here? Tell a depressed person there is no hope and you are confirming that person's belief system. And pushing her deeper into hell, hopelessness, and despair. You are telling her that her reality of despair is the ultimate.

Can the world truly be that awful? Logically, I can answer in the affirmative. And there's lots of supporting evidence. But my heart can't stand that. It cries, "No! The ultimate isn't hopelessness."

I want to help you understand how hell can be and not be at the same time. How hell can be your home and not exist. That raises a tough question. When hell ceases to exist, what happens to its inhabitants? To us? It's quite simple. We cease to exist, too.

A couple hundred years ago, during the time of the Enlightenment, people in the Western world became convinced that material reality, the tangible, was the only reality. Those angels, devils, God, the Voice of Aloneness, were all unreal. By decree. They said, in effect, "If we can't see it, if you can't demonstrate it to us under a microscope, then it doesn't exist. *Show* us God or an angel or a dream, and we will let them be."

This puts us in a hell of a predicament. What we are feeling, our depression and despair about the nature of things, is defined away. Our questions aren't considered *real* questions. See? The materialist tells us why: "It's because you're believing what isn't true. Only the tangible is real."

Let's enter the argument with the materialist. Try to get a hearing for ourselves. Maybe that will free us from the hell of isolation. If we can share with another how awful it is to be defined away. Let's cry out, "But you don't understand. We *know* the reality of it. We are caught in hell. If you would believe in hell, you could help free us."

"You're crazy. Show me hell or I won't believe it."

See? There is nowhere to go in the argument. You *are* showing him hell. But since it isn't tangible, a physical place he can step into, he won't even consider its reality. Instead, hell is declared nonexistent and is not *allowed* to exist. The Voice of Aloneness is thus a voice from nowhere that proves you're crazy. Your one possible avenue to something better is declared unreal. By a *view* of reality. By a view that refuses to *see* the nonmaterial. If I'm honest, I have to admit there is a materialist in me who agrees. The argument about what is the nature of reality is going on inside me. And you.

Don't accept that materialistic view as the true picture of reality. Instead, trust your depression. Trust the cry of unhappiness and anguish in you. Trust the Voice of Aloneness that says, "You're no good, you're a lying, petty jerk." It's better than being nothing. Honestly.

But what a painful counter to nonexistence I'm offering! "Rejoice, folks. Hell exists. Fear not."

Yes. Hell exists. The Voice of Aloneness speaks. We are moving toward reality. Which we are told doesn't exist. Do you see that I am expressing a different view of reality when I say this? That I am believing something different than the materialists?

But maybe they're right. Maybe none of this real. Maybe. But if they are right, then we're trapped. Nowhere.

I remember a woman whose lover had deserted her a few months earlier. She was stuck in her grief. Every suggestion, thought, memory, and possibility brought her back to her misery. When I asked her what her stuckness was like, she said it felt as if she were stuck in mud. Her wheels were spinning, couldn't grip the mud. She couldn't get out of that mudhole no matter how much energy she used. I asked her how she'd get out of mud in real life.

"I'd call a tow truck," she said simply.

"Let a tow truck pull you out then," I answered her seriously.

She burst out laughing. It was a ridiculous suggestion. All our talking and weeping had gotten nowhere. Or more truly, our talking and weeping had recognized the hell she was in. The tow truck pulled her out of the mud. It moved her. She got out of that mudhole and trudged on. She made it, by the way, out of hell. Which is probably the only way we make it. By the way.

But we haven't convinced the materialists, have we? Nor will we, in all likelihood. But it may help us to consider another view, radically different from materialism, which states that materialists shouldn't be so cocky about their tangible reality.

Based on my college experience, I choose to call this the Krishna maneuver. Simply declare *them* unreal. As Krishna did in the Bhagavad Gita. Imagine with me a conversation with the Hindu god Krishna. Listen in as Krishna talks to the warrior Arjuna.

"It's all right to kill them, Arjuna. They aren't real. The material world isn't real. It is *maya,* a beautiful dance of illusion. It doesn't exist. You don't need to listen. Or worry about them because they aren't real."

At first, Krishna's words are soothing. We use them as a counter-attack. Until a horrible concern surfaces. I ask Krishna the question, "And I? Am *I* real?"

Krishna turns to me and says, "Ultimately, you aren't real either. Hell isn't real, nor is heaven. Your depression isn't real. The Voice of Aloneness isn't real. Only the Absolute is real and you go to it when you die. You dissolve into the Absolute like a drop into the ocean. Be at peace."

"Yikes!" is my response to the offer of peace. Because dissolving into the Absolute doesn't bring me peace. Material reality, then, becomes a sinkhole. And worse, my friends, my loved ones, and I, myself, fall into the sinkhole. We don't matter. It makes the walls shimmer. Reality wobbles on the edge of dissolution. I fear that dissolution leads to Halloween, not to bliss.

Krishna's words don't help me, or you. For some people, dissolving into bliss, into unity with the Absolute, will bring peace. Not for me. Which is perhaps an indication of my unenlightened state. Fine. Here is my response to what I hear from Krishna.

To the statement that my loved ones don't matter, "No!"

To the statement that matter doesn't exist, is only illusion, "No! Matter matters."

To the statement that my being is illusion, that the Voice of Aloneness is illusion, "No! I'd rather throw my arms around the Voice of Aloneness than believe that." Though the romance no doubt will be short-lived, what with the constant, "You're no good, You're a liar." It wears on a person.

Here is a third view of reality. *All* of it is real. The ground, the trees, the stars, buildings, heaven, hell, the Voice of Aloneness, Another Alone. You aren't crazy. You are facing reality. Your depression is literally that. You have been depressing reality, pressing reality down because you fell for materialism. Matter is real. But psyche is real, too. Halloween is real. The spirit is real.

This view settles me. It acknowledges hell, that place through which we are moving. It acknowledges the Voice of Aloneness, says we're not crazy to listen to it. It acknowledges the possibility of Another Alone. But doesn't guarantee it. Though it admits that it makes sense. It could be so. It's certainly worth a look.

Each of these views is a valid view of reality and, to a degree, self-determining. If, for instance, I name hell as illusion, I take away my power to deal with it. I isolate it. It becomes unreal.

Sort of. There is our depression still calling us, saying there's got to be more. If we make no place for some part of reality, does it find other ways to make itself known? Wobble the walls for a materialist and you're messing with his fundament. If the walls can wobble, what? Let me tell you, there is no comfort for the materialist in the chant, "I'm crazy, I'm crazy, I'm crazy."

It's certainly obvious that the inclusive view is the one that speaks to me. In one sense, I was a materialist who was cast out of my materialist reality. That reality crumbled for me. The material world was the only reality, then like Humpty Dumpty, the whole world cracked into little pieces. But Krishna's words left me empty, too. I didn't merge with the Absolute. I was submerged into a deeper reality, without a clue how to make my way in it. Then came connectedness, my isolation seen. That crazy cross which raises eighty-seven more questions. It touched me, though.

CLAIMING REALITY

This is what I think about reality, fellow hell-bound isolated ones. What we believe about reality has a tremendous effect on how reality shows itself to us. The Voice of Aloneness attacks our blindness and denial of inner reality. Cries out to us with this much truth. Our separate realities are pushing into other realities that will show us Reality. By hook or by crook. By depression, if necessary. Mephistopheles again, that part of evil that forever works the good. In one sense, yes. It works the good because the fabric of the universe, reality, is *more than* the material only, is *more than* the self only, is *more than* the spiritual only.

Just because some aspect of reality doesn't give us the whole picture doesn't mean it isn't real. It means it isn't *all* of reality.

It's all right not to know everything. It's all right to live in a mysterious universe. It's even all right that there is hell. But only if there is Another Alone who is calling to each of us wherever we are.

I want to share something that I wrote in my journal recently about this. I was dialoguing with Another Alone about the stuff of this book, with all that writing this book stirs up in me. Like hell. I was struggling with hell. Here's part of the dialogue.

ANOTHER ALONE (A) (in response to my soul complaints and struggles): *It is hard for you to be in Halloween and hell again. To open it, to learn there.*
ME: *Yes.*
A: *To see messages written on the walls of hell since the beginning for you.*
ME: *Touches me. Tell me.*
A: *Hell, walking through it. Messages are there so you can find your way. Love. Love in hell.*
ME: *As though you always knew I'd go to hell.*
A: *As though I put markers everywhere for you.*

Stepping away from this piece of dialogue now. What if this is true? What if Another Alone is everywhere for me? What if every path is marked? What would that say about reality? About possibility?

What if every path is marked for you? What if you can't be lost even though you're lost? Does this make any sense to you? More importantly, does it seem possible? Imagine that there are messages near you now that want to lead you on. Do you feel excited? A sense of hope? Frustration?

To recapitulate:

One View of Reality: It is only a material world. Whatever is nonmaterial isn't real. Don't worry about it. You're just crazy. Come back home to your little meaningless life. You will forget your questions. You will relax. Come. Come home.

A Second View of Reality: Only the Absolute is real. You and the rest of the ten thousand things are not real. Your depression is not real. Your friends are not real. Find peace. Dissolve into the cosmic ocean.

A Third View of Reality: Life is a journey. Matter, spirit, persons. All these are real. There is the Voice of Aloneness and Another Alone who longs to guide you. Who seeks to bring you home to a place you've never been.

You may know something of the truth of each of these realities. They bring you to three different homes. Here we are embarked on the third way. Come along if this way offers you hope.

5

IMAGINATION

If reality includes the nonmaterial world, how are we to enter it? How are we to encounter it? How are we to relate to it? The answer is perhaps obvious to you. We use the imagination. That is what we have been doing already. We followed Dante through the dark wood into hell. We listened to the Voice of Aloneness. We pictured Another Alone. The woman stuck in mud called a tow truck. All this is imagery. This is quite a suggestion. Imagination is our avenue to inner reality.

Do you believe that imagination can connect you to reality? Or is imagination imaginary to you? Does it help you to escape reality rather than to enter it? Perhaps the claim that imagination leads to reality pushes you toward depression again. Perhaps it seems a made-up solution.

These are legitimate concerns. We need to address them right now. I want to take you into the imagination lab. Remember high school biology? The first time you saw a worm lying in a tray in front of you? How did you feel? Were you excited, afraid? Opening up that creature taught you something that description alone could not. So, too, with the imagination. When you find yourself isolated, you will want to have strategies for dealing with your isolation.

Enter with me now on an extended dialogue with the inner skeptic. You probably know the skeptic's voice well. It is an expression of the Voice of Aloneness. It speaks of the impossibility of hope. And it hides something of great value at its center. Something we can get to only by entering deeply into our skeptical nature. But we don't want to be swallowed by our skepticism. We want to dialogue with it as other. Come with me now on a search for the great value hidden in skepticism.

A DIALOGUE WITH THE SKEPTIC

ME: *Greetings, skeptic. I come to talk with you about the value of imagination.*

SKEPTIC: *Seems to me that just a minute ago you were talking about reality.*

ME: *I was.*

SKEPTIC: *Where did reality go?*

ME: *Imagination carries reality.*

SKEPTIC: *No it doesn't. Imagination avoids reality.*

ME: *I disagree. I believe that imagination makes reality.*

SKEPTIC: *So everything is real including the stuff you make up, huh?*

ME: *Listen closely. Imagination isn't "made up." It is real. When you were a little kid did you fantasize?*

SKEPTIC: *Sure.*

ME: *Imagine all kind of things?*

SKEPTIC: *Yeah.*

ME: *Did they come true?*

SKEPTIC: *That's just what I'm talking about. I imagined stuff that never came true, that couldn't come true. Now you bring me down into this place you tell me is hell and have me start looking at my isolation. I start to feel hopeful, like this crummy depression doesn't have to last forever, then you tell me this.*

ME: *What's upsetting you?*

SKEPTIC: *This imaginary stuff. You're going to make up some solution. How stupid do you think I am? I admitted to you how awful I feel sometimes, how isolated, and you tell me this.*

ME: *I never said imaginary. I said imagination. There's a difference.*

SKEPTIC: *Big difference. To be honest with you, I feel worse than when we started.*

ME: *Would you agree that what we've said so far is true? That you are, in fact, isolated? That it feels like hell? That calling it hell in some ways helped you?*

SKEPTIC: *Yeah. It helped me back there. For a minute anyway.*

ME: *You were already feeling the effects of the imagination. Images were touching you, exposing you to your hurt, sparking hope. We've been using images a lot already. Like hell. That's an image. The Voice of Aloneness is an image. That tow truck is an image. Remember? It got that woman unstuck.*

SKEPTIC: *Yeah. So?*

(A typical skeptical remark, isn't it? The skeptic opens up a little. Then is dragged back into skepticism. It is a fearful thing to give up our skepticism. Skepticism keeps us safely miserable, unexposed.)

ME: *You're a materialist.*

SKEPTIC: *What?*

ME: *You think that images aren't real because you can't see them. Because they arise out of the mysterious darkness inside you. Because they have no weight. Deep down you think that only tangible things are real.*

SKEPTIC: *Maybe. I have come this far with you. I'm not a total skeptic even if I'm a fool.*

ME: *I feel an opening in you. Let me tell you a true story that happened around 1950. Was written up in scientific journals. There was a guy who got terminal cancer, had developed a huge tumor, at the time the drug Krebiozen was being tested. Doctors thought that Krebiozen might be the new miracle cancer drug. This man's doctor gave him the medicine and his tumor disappeared rapidly.*

SKEPTIC: *That's easy. It was a miracle drug.*

ME: *Nope. When the data came in, Krebiozen was shown to provide no medical benefit.*

SKEPTIC: *Then what was it? Spontaneous remission? I have friends who have gotten better unexplainably.*

ME: *As soon as the results were made public, the guy's tumor came back.*

SKEPTIC: *So? Coincidence.*

ME: *His doctor gave him a pill that had no medicine in it. Told him it was super-strength Krebiozen. Much better than the other stuff.*

SKEPTIC: *And?*

ME: *He got better immediately.*

SKEPTIC: *That's weird.*

ME: *It gets weirder. When later the papers announced that Krebiozen had absolutely no value, the guy's tumor came back full force and he was dead in a couple days. Something is going on here. What the guy expects to happen does happen.*

Imagination. You see how powerful it is. Healed him twice, then killed him.

SKEPTIC: *His cancer killed him.*

ME: *His imagination, his expectation, played a role.*

SKEPTIC: *A fluke.*

ME: *Maybe. You've heard stories about women who lift cars off trapped children?*

SKEPTIC: *Yeah, I've heard stories like that.*

ME: *How do you explain them?*

SKEPTIC: *They were desperate. Their kids were in danger. They had no choice but to lift those cars.*

ME: *Listen to yourself. They did the impossible. They lifted cars off their kids. Couldn't do it later. How do you explain it?*

SKEPTIC: *Adrenaline. How do I know? They were desperate.*

ME : *Maybe you're onto something. Maybe when a person is desperate, the impossible has a better chance of happening. Like someone who is in hell, depressed, trapped, with the nothing dissolving everything. The nothing is gobbling it up, the Voice of Aloneness, hell, you. But it doesn't gobble up the depression. The depression gets worse when the nothing is finished, when the nothing is all that remains.*

SKEPTIC: *Except the depression.*

(Observe that the skeptic and I have come to a point of agreement. About depression. Also observe that the skeptic's questions are opening *me*. Changing my attitude).

ME: *The nothing fails to gobble up the depression. In fact, it feeds it. Or seems to. Because the depression gets stronger. More insistent. Hopelessness deepens. A deep chill sets in. Your soul aches even more. Isolation is so complete even hell won't have it.*

SKEPTIC: *Right.*

ME: *But there's that pesty depression. It grows. The nothing tries to gobble it up. Fails. The depression grows.*

SKEPTIC: *Like a tumor.*

ME: *Or a plant.*

SKEPTIC: *Feels more like a tumor to me. A sickness unto death. Some people kill themselves it hurts so bad.*

ME: *Because it's so real.*

SKEPTIC: *Yeah.*

ME: *That even the nothing can't handle it.*

SKEPTIC: *You aren't helping me.*

ME: *There is something greater than the nothing, than that which has no images. Depression.*

SKEPTIC: *What kind of world is this if only depression can withstand the nothing? Not a universe I want to occupy.*

ME: *I agree with you. If depression is the only thing that can survive the nothing, we're left with something very much like hell. But there is something else that can survive the nothing. At least sometimes.*

SKEPTIC: *What?*

ME: *Desperation.*

SKEPTIC: *Oh great.*

ME: *Desperation has been known to lift cars.*

SKEPTIC: *Like the wind in a hurricane.*

ME: *Now you're beginning to get it. Maybe desperation is like the wind. Maybe when it gets blowing really hard it lifts cars off kids.*

SKEPTIC: *Or destroys things.*

ME: *Some things need to be destroyed. To make room for new possibilities. That's what happens when an old building gets knocked down by a wrecking ball. An architect is hired, a plan for a new building is drawn up and accepted, a wrecking crew goes to the site and destroys the old building, a new building is built. Imagination.*

SKEPTIC: *Imagination?*

ME: *If the architect hadn't designed it, if the people with the money couldn't envision it, the old building would still be there. Remember Michelangelo?*

SKEPTIC: *I'm all ears.*

ME: *He took a stone. Saw a sculpture in the stone. Set out to free what was trapped there. Did a pretty good job, too.*

Skeptic: *Yeah, he did.*

ME: *Nuclear bombs. Never could have blown up those two cities if a bunch of desperate scientists, desperate smart scientists, hadn't imagined it. They discovered a power locked in reality.*

SKEPTIC: *Used it to kill.*

ME: *I'm not talking morality here. Just fact. The fact is that without images nothing new happens. Nothing is discovered. No questions are asked of life.*

SKEPTIC: *Used it to kill thousands of people. Kaboom. Just like*

*that. Nothinged them. What do you say about that? Imagination
can bring the nothing.*

(Do you sense the passion of the skeptic? Perhaps it is that
passion that makes it so skeptical.)

ME: *Yes. Imagination is very powerful.*

SKEPTIC: *Even if I grant that, imagination isn't trustworthy. It
can be used to destroy, to nothing.*

ME: *We've moved some, haven't we? Suddenly imagination
seems very real, too real. It kills. It knocks down buildings. It
destroys cities. It may be too hot for us to handle. At the least, we
must respect it. Another strange idea occurs to me, a hell of an
idea. Suppose that there is a force that wants to nothing the
world. Suppose it has the power to uncreate, to use imagination
to destroy. Suppose that imagination isn't bad, or good for that
matter. That imagination is a power. A different kind of reality
that can be tapped into and used. For good or ill. And this force is
using it to destroy.*

SKEPTIC: *Very depressing. Scary. Makes me feel small,
hopeless.*

ME: *The Voice of Aloneness says, "Give it up. It's hopeless.
You're a puny being who can be rubbed out of existence with the
snap of a finger. No matter what you do this will happen. Ultimately you become nothing because, as you suspected, life is an
echthros." You've seen the bumper sticker, "Life sucks and then
you die."*

SKEPTIC: *Smart philosopher wrote that.*

ME: *The Voice of Aloneness draining your life blood, sinking
you into your depression, into desperation, if you've got any
energy left. You open to your depression as though to nothing.
That is what life offers according to the Voice of Aloneness.
Nothing. Those are the facts. The Voice is just serving life.
Getting rid of a little piece of it—you—as life does. Making quick
business, of you at least. Only life keeps happening, keeps
refusing to go away. Like there really is Another Alone imagining it. Something that seems to believe that nothing isn't everything. Another Alone doesn't serve the nothing. Another Alone
serves life.*

SKEPTIC: *But it loses.*

ME: *Maybe. The spring comes every year.*

SKEPTIC: *But me. But people starving. But cancer. But earth-*

quakes and droughts. But murder. But drug addiction. But despair. But the screams of desperation. Where is this Another Alone?

ME: *In the middle of it, wailing.*

SKEPTIC: *Wailing? That's a sorry excuse for help. That's admitting defeat.*

ME: *It's not admitting anything. Wailing is opening. You should try it some time.*

SKEPTIC: *It wouldn't help.*

ME: *So you imagine.*

SKEPTIC: *I'm getting angry. I'd like to tell you to take a hike.*

ME: *We're taking one. Through hell. Remember? You're feeling hell. You're suffering. You're looking at the hopelessness, feeling it in your bones. You are a good person. I heard your cry for everyone and everything.*

SKEPTIC: *My futile cry.*

ME: *No. Don't define it. Name it. It is the cry of your soul. It is your being responding to the power that nothings. Protesting. Yelling your desperation.*

SKEPTIC: *Hopeless.*

ME: *You don't know that it's hopeless.*

SKEPTIC: *Look around. We're in hell. People are starving, hurting, dying.*

ME: *The only way out is to walk through here. You couldn't walk up that mountain straight to heaven, could you?*

SKEPTIC: *No.*

ME: *Do you want me to tell you why? It's because you know you've got no business in heaven so long as these others are in hell. You can't feast while they starve. I'm afraid if you let yourself, you, too, will become a broken bodhisattva. I'm getting to you, aren't I? I see a great sadness in your face.*

SKEPTIC: *Yes.*

ME: *A sadness that wells up in your belly.*

SKEPTIC: *Yes.*

ME: *You are one of the starving ones.*

SKEPTIC: *Yes.*

ME: *You can feel the hunger of your soul gnawing at you. Refusing to go out of existence.*

SKEPTIC: *Yes.*

ME: *You can hear the cries of others and you have nothing to offer them.*

SKEPTIC: (Doesn't answer.)

ME: *Nothing to offer yourself. Except imagination. Is it pos-sible that imagination would serve the good? That imagination is the pivot point of reality? Think of it. Everything ever made by human beings is a product of the imagination. Good or bad, it comes from the imagination. Imagination makes reality. Try another depressing image. Smog, pollution, the outcome of an encounter between imagination and fossil fuels. A different imagination wants to change this, wants to clean up the world.*

SKEPTIC: *And it is failing. Whole species are disappearing.*

ME: *I have a hard question for you. Which will you serve? The nothing or Another Alone? Imagination is making reality either way. Making it into nothing. Or creating life. Which one will you serve? Choose. You must. To quote Isaac Bashevis Singer, "We must believe in free will. We have no choice." Choose. You can't choose not to choose because that's to choose the nothing. To give in to the nothing. To serve the nothing by becoming nothing.*

SKEPTIC: *You're starting to anger me again.*

ME: *Good. Then there's hope. I would much rather anger you into fighting me than have you serve the nothing. Your anger tells me that there is life in you.*

SKEPTIC: *Futile life.*

ME: *So you choose to serve the nothing.*

SKEPTIC: *Aieii! You're driving me crazy.*

ME: *Just asking you to open. And you're doing it. Despera-tion. Compassion for the needy. Anger. There's life in you, I tell you. Choose it.*

SKEPTIC: *How?*

ME: *By being where you are. By imagining it. By opening to Another Alone.*

SKEPTIC: *Hear my cry. I don't believe in Another Alone though I long for it. Hear my cry. I am isolated, lost, hopeless. Hear my cry. The nothing has hold of me. Even though I long for life, the nothing has me. Hear my cry. I want help. I just don't believe in it. I long for it. I am opening, ripping open. But I find only vacancy and pain. The encroachment of the nothing. Hear my cry. Hear my cry. You do something. I am crying out to you. You want images? I am drowning. I am going under. I am beyond my last breath. I have no energy left. My life is seeping out of me. I am the starving child. I am the tortured prisoner. I am the dying one. I am despair. It is over. Can you not hear that? Over. I am going down. Forever. Depression is not a good enough response to the nothing. Even if it is the cry of Another Alone. Another Alone is losing me. Do you hear? If there is anything you can do, do it now. Soon you will look for me and I will be gone. Gone. To Sheol. To hell. To nothingness. And yet I cry, I yell, I bellow. To what? To whom? To the great nothing which devours my sounds. You have touched me. I am crying out. Help me. Help me. Bring Another Alone to me. Let it find me. I am drowning. Going under. Being engulfed in the blackness.*

A Quiet Voice speaks: I will help you. I hear your cry. I am Another Alone. Listen, child, to these stories. Listen and begin to find your life.

6

STORIES

Stories hold the world together. People have always told each other stories. Preliterate tribes gathered around campfires at night and listened to the stories of their tribes. Of their origins, of their ancestral heroes, of their place in the universe. Children thrive on stories. "Tell me about the day I was born, Daddy. I want to hear that one again." "Read me *Goodnight, Moon* again [for the seventy-fourth night in a row], Mommy." "Remember when I caught that fish? It was squirming all over the boat. I love that one. Tell it to me again."

Stories tell us again that the world is meaningful. That the world holds together. That we have a place in it. That we are part of the world's story. Hearing these stories over and over again makes us know we belong.

What are anniversaries but times when we remember the stories of significant events? A marriage, a graduation, a death. So that we can celebrate it again. So that we can call it back into existence and feel its power again.

What do we do at night on camping trips? We sit around the campfire like our ancestors did and tell stories. Or when we visit friends from the past? We recount the stories of our youth together. And if the story comes back to life, we are, if only for a moment, reconnected again. How terrible it feels when a memory falls flat, for we are left isolated and sad, cut off from our friends. Because the memory has failed to become a story.

We are hungry for stories. Novels, plays, movies, and situation comedies on television are all stories. Imagine turning on your favorite television program. On this particular episode, the characters are acting in unfamiliar ways. The normally bigoted father is holding a party honoring his black neighbor. The kind son is doing everything in his power to ruin the party. The mother who always resolves the family's problems is baying at the moon. This would upset you because the characters aren't being true to themselves. And this ruins the story.

ENTERING THE STORY

Stories bring coherence to the happenings of life. Stories make something of the world. They contain power. They give life. They connect us. We are lost without stories. Life loses its meaning. Without stories, we are isolated. We approach the nothing. We are grabbed by the Voice of Aloneness, who says the same words over and over again: "You're no good. You're petty. You're a liar." Which isn't a story. It is a condemnation to isolation.

If stories connect us, what about stories in hell? What can connect us in hell? What images can break the isolation? For that's the only hope in hell, isn't it? That our stories will connect us. Free us. Not push us further under.

Recall the cry of the skeptic at the end of the last chapter. "I am drowning. I am going under. I am beyond my last breath." Did these words capture you? Did they touch you? Did your feelings stir for the skeptic? Mine did. And Another Alone spoke. Invited the skeptic to listen to stories and thereby find life. Here is a story. A woman takes an ocean cruise. She falls overboard and drowns. End of story. That's not much of a story, is it? Why doesn't it work? Because you know nothing about her. You don't care about her. Your fantasy isn't activated at all, is it? These few words about her haven't connected you to her.

Let's flesh out the story now with some images and see what happens. A woman has worked for years with emotionally disabled children. She has saved her nickels and dimes diligently because she wants to take a Caribbean cruise. Finally, after years of saving, she is able to purchase her ticket and embark on her journey. The first three days of the cruise are wonderful. On the third evening she dances with a lovely man and feels hope stirring inside her heart as she drifts into sleep. "Maybe he'll call me when we get back home," she thinks. "Maybe we'll see each other. Maybe . . ."

The ship's siren startles her awake two hours later. She pulls on her robe, and rushes to the deck where people are frantically climbing into lifeboats. Only now does she smell the smoke. She thinks of her dance partner. She wants to warn him, but has no idea where his room is. By now the smoke prohibits her searching for him. A great feeling of despair engulfs her. Suddenly an explosion causes the boat to shudder, throwing her overboard. All around her people are crying for help. But she can't help them, nor herself, for she doesn't know how to swim. She sinks into the ocean and the water closes over her.

If I have succeeded at all, the second version at least interests you. The images tell you something about the woman. They help you care about her. She's on her first cruise. On the last night of her life, there comes the possibility of a romance. And then she is thrown overboard and disappears in the black ocean. What if she had lived? Would the two of them have gotten together? Did the man die in the explosion?

Well, let's see. Let's allow the story to continue. Mr. Smith, erstwhile dancer and former Olympic swimmer, has seen her go under. He leaps into the water and swims toward her, each stroke pulling him closer to her. Mr. Smith had given up swimming years earlier because his wife preferred tennis. He had resumed swimming laps at the local club just two months ago after his wife's untimely and remarkable death. While standing at net, she was hit in the neck by a smash shot that damaged her windpipe. Unable to breathe, she died in minutes. Drowned, you might say.

His strong arms quickly erase the distance between them. His eyes never leave the spot where she has gone down. Finally he is there. He dives into the deeps. But he can't find her. It is too dark.

Just then her robe drifts across his face. He wraps his arm around her, lifts her to the surface, and drags her toward a lifeboat, which has room for two more people. He pushes her onto the boat, follows her in. Their lips meet and he resuscitates her. The ship moves toward New York, toward marriage, toward bliss.

I know the ending is kind of cornball. But it's better, don't you agree, than her drowning?

The skeptic is drowning. The skeptic in you is drowning from your depression and hopelessness. Where is that Olympic swimmer? Is he coming toward you? Or is the imagery just too unrealistic for you? Do I anger you with this corny story? Am I not taking your drowning seriously?

Let me assure you that I am. That whole story grows out of concern for you. I want you to be able to imagine that someone can be saved from drowning. Just start there. If you can imagine that, maybe you can begin to write your own story. Maybe in your story you'll remember your child who needs you and with one last heroic effort swim to the surface to live another day. Maybe an arm will reach into the water and rescue you. Maybe you'll remember the time you almost did drown. When the undertow got you. Or a wave knocked you over and threw you under water. Or someone at the pool held you under so long that you thought you were going to die.

Once again, the Voice of Aloneness speaks. "What is this garbage? These stories about being saved? They are fanciful and foolish, which is exactly what stories are, friend. Just stories. Lies."

Here is the same charge we heard about imagination. The Voice claims that stories are imaginary, unreal. But worse, the Voice calls the storyteller a liar. Feel how disempowering the following sentence is. That was only a story. Only. That word makes a story into a lie. And creates another story that says that stories are only stories. That the true story is that there is no story. And that's the story. But why should *that* story be considered true? How do we know *it* isn't a lie? What if we act like it is the truth, and it isn't? Tragically, it then can become true. If you fall into the water and *know* you can't be saved, you may give up even though help is on the way. Help comes too late because you didn't try to stay afloat.

I disagree with the Voice of Aloneness. Stories aren't lies. They help us imagine the possible. You can sometimes say about a story, "That isn't so." But what if, instead, you asked, "Could it be so?" When you do that you are opening to story, opening to surprise, allowing the inbreaking of the new.

Hell banishes the new. The Voice of Aloneness says, "There is no new. When are you going to accept that and move toward the nothing?"

Our best answer to that is, "Never! I will never accept that there is no possibility of the new."

Am I storytelling now? Am I lying? Or at least denying what has brought us here? What *has* brought us here? First the skeptic cried, "I'm drowning!" Then Another Alone told us to open to stories. Then I created the above story about the cruise. Its function was to suggest the possibility of being saved from drowning, to separate us for a moment from our own drowning, to hint that we may not have to be swallowed up by our hellish troubles.

But now we must attend directly to our own needs. We need stories that connect to us. In hell. Isolation stories. Sadly, I know hundreds, though happily, most of them don't end in isolation.

It always annoyed me as a child when a story ended with the words: "And they lived happily ever after." Like the situation comedy, this ending doesn't satisfy. It feels like "happily ever after" means that nothing exciting ever happened again. There were no more challenges. The story just peters out. Runs out of gas.

People who get through isolation do so by entering life, by entering the story of their lives. They don't want a cosmic happily-everafter. They want to get through this particular situation. That's what story does. It takes on a particular situation, like drowning, and moves with it, considering various possibilities. This is a wonderful and frightening thing. To use the example of the cruise, the woman could have drowned, or could have been saved but brain-damaged because she was under water too long. She could have fallen in love with the man. Or he could have disappeared from her life, etc. Images can tell the good or the bad story. Those of us in hell want our bad stories to have good endings.

A TRUE STORY ABOUT ALMOST DROWNING

Good friends of mine lost their ten-year-old son to cancer several years ago. It was a long and painful illness that brought them to several cities seeking a cure. After his death, they took a muchneeded vacation together to recuperate from their long ordeal. They arrived at their destination and settled into their hotel room on the tenth floor. One night the husband had a dream in which he was standing in a great bog that he knew was his own inner evil. He couldn't run from it, couldn't escape it. When he awoke, a voice spoke. "Why don't you go to the balcony and jump?" (We know this voice, don't we?) The voice persisted, "Go ahead, jump, you won't hurt yourself. The trees will catch you." Then again, "Jump into the pool." Finally, it said to him, "If you jump, you will see your son." When he resisted, the voice began to scream, "Jump! Jump! Jump!" And then calmly, "Why don't you go out on the balcony and sit?" After two hours, he woke his wife. When her arms wrapped around him, the attack ceased immediately.

Now *there* is a story. One we would never have heard if he had followed the advice of the Voice of Aloneness. It would have been a story with a tragic ending. My friend would be dead, a suicide. Possibilities. The horrible possibility of listening to the Voice of Aloneness and leaping to his death. From desire to be with his son. The wonderful possibility that happened. He didn't jump. He made a connection with his wife. Relationship rescued him. Ultimately, they adopted another son.

Do I take you seriously? Oh yes. I don't want you to drown. I want you to be rescued. I don't want you to leap to your death. I want you to live happily ever after. How about that? The story of my friend changes me again. If the choice is between drowning and living happily ever after, I want you to live happily ever after. Though experience tells me that "They lived happily ever after" would be stated better thus: "They got a little rest after their adventure. And then they went on to new adventures."

I'm thinking of my children. Of reading them stories when they were little. Of wanting them to get tired so they'd go to sleep. I can hear them say when I suggested that there were new adventures "What adventures, Dad? Where did they go next? Tell me that one."

But right there is my problem with "happily ever after." The phrase suggests to me a story ending. Another Alone, if I may speak for it (and somebody has to, maybe *all* of us do), wants the story to begin, not to end. Wants the drowning to open to new life. They lived happily ever after means that they *lived*. That there are more stories to tell about them. Do you see? When I take "happily ever after" to mean the story is over, isolation begins again. Because they are gone.

But, stories don't have to finish. Watch this. A woman dies of breast cancer. Is buried. A few friends remember her. They die. The story dies. Finished.

Now watch this. The same woman dies of breast cancer. One of her friends is frightened enough to see a doctor, who removes a breast lump, malignant, before it kills her. She lives several more years, in fact takes care of her grandson whose parents are drug addicts. He finds his way to college, becomes a surgeon. Helps people by removing their tumors which would otherwise kill them.

I've done it again. Taken a few images and opened a story of possibility. Very quickly, a possible story occurred to me. If that can happen in my mind, why can't it happen in life?

Let me stretch this further, simply because my imagination is able to. The woman who died in the first story entered another dimension where she embarked on great adventures that, incidentally, helped this young man so he did not become a drug addict. I know I'm just imagining, making up a story. I'm trying to show you that a story can go anywhere. Do you get that? *Anywhere*. Even into our skeptic's drowning. The skeptic doesn't have to drown. And even if the skeptic does die, the story doesn't have to end. Imagine that, will you? Get enough sense of the reality of story to see that story never ends. It can fabricate.

The Voice of Aloneness intrudes: "Yes. You mean lie."

I mean fabricate. As in weaving a meaningful tale. As in creating something. As in making something new. As in not drowning. Weaving, fabricating a story can save a life.

"Jump! Jump! Jump!" That's what we're up against. I know it. The Voice of Aloneness was screaming at my friend. He could have jumped. It is amazing that he didn't. And do you see what changed everything? After two hours—think of it—he finally stepped out of his isolation. He imagined another possibility in his great aloneness. He asked his wife to hold him. She wrapped her arms around him. Took the little orphan to her and loved him. That's what we need.

A STORY OF INNER SURGERY

One more story. And to quote (accurately, I think) from an old television program, "There are eight million stories in the naked city." Everybody has a story, a never-ending story. This particular story involves an imagined surgery.

Recently, radical surgery happened in my office. A woman who had been struggling for over a year to free herself to be real, and not so blasted nice all the time, got to the point where she needed to open up. She felt lost, despairing, that she had tried everything— and maybe she had. There was a sense of hopelessness in the middle of her belly. She felt it sucking the life right out of her. "There's nothing more to do. I've exhausted all possibilities. I'm doomed to this awful belly pain and hopelessness."

I asked her to imagine surgery being done on her belly to discover what was causing her such pain. She closed her eyes, took some deep breaths, then at my suggestion, called in a surgeon, whom she identified as a midwife. The midwife took a knife, slit her open, and found a large, black mass in her womb. It had connected itself to her with a thousand tentacles. Slowly, using the knife, the midwife cut each tentacle. The pain was not extreme, felt instead like a razor nick. Finally, all the tentacles were cut. The midwife lifted the mass from her, threw it aside, then sewed up the woman's belly. When I suggested she might want to put it in a sealed container, to inhibit its power to reattach to her, she agreed. I asked if she wanted to say anything to the midwife. "Yes, I want to ask her for a relationship with a man." She frowned as she did so.

"What is it?" I asked.

"She said I'm not ready for a relationship. And I believe her."

We closed the imaginative exercise with her picturing a chalice as a symbol of wholeness, as a container for her soul. Her story had a powerful effect on me, but less so on her. Although it made sense to her in principle, she wasn't touched deeply in her feeling self.

At our next meeting, she told me that she had been struggling since our last session. She found herself blocking out not only the tentacled thing, but also positive comments and feelings from her friends. As I listened, I saw something creative happening. She was shutting out the good as well as the bad. Which in her case, curiously, was a positive thing.

This woman had given her early life to serving her mother's depression. She had only managed to escape when she was in her twenties by giving her life to God, by saying to herself, "I belong to God. I am not this body, this mind, this spirit. I am God's." Now that no longer worked. She had connected to her body. Had found the tentacled thing, which she believed was her mother's depression, living there. She saw herself in danger on both sides. Of being overwhelmed by the negativity she'd received from her mother. Of disembodying herself by listening to her caring friends. She *needed* to feel the pain in her belly. She needed to feel her body. She needed to enter into her body-self and be. Another image came. She saw herself between two fences which protected her from depression and disembodiment. That told her where she needed to be. Safe for now, between the fences.

To be with her, I had to enter her story. It made no sense to try to force her to be in a "positive" place. That would have isolated her from her body-being. Again, we're not talking "happily ever after" here. We're talking about stepping into the middle of a person's ongoing story.

AN EXERCISE

Is it true that we are all in the middle of our stories? That we are all longing to tell our stories to someone who can hear us and free us from our isolation? Or better, to step into it with us? I think we are. I think we all want to have someone to wake up when we're desperate. Someone to whom we can cry, "Hold me!" Or, "I'm drowning!"

Stories are lives not lies. Stories are tales of who we are and who we long to be. Stories are happening. If you drown, that's the story. If you somehow manage to swim to safety, that's the story. If someone reaches into the water and drags you out, that's the story. The story is happening. The point is that there is more than one possible story line. Even if you drown.

I want to challenge you now, to urge you to enter into the middle of your story. I want you to go into your drowning and let the story unfold. I want you to forget the drowning if that isn't your image. Find *your* image. Find the story that is moving in you. Step into it. Become part of it. Dare to let happen whatever your inner being wants to happen. But do one thing. This is all I ask of you. Find some way to share your story. Even if you're embarrassed. Find someone to tell. If you can find no other, let your story be a part of this book. Imagine me hearing it. Entering into your story of isolation with you. After all, you've done the same for me. This is the great news that I keep harping about. You're not alone, even if you are. You can let one of us into your loneliness. There is Another Alone who listens to each of us, who brings us together. That's what I believe. That's the way my story is unfolding.

What is this? Am I writing you into my story? Am I not letting you be as isolated as you are? It is time for you to get busy, to say what story you want for your life, so it can come to be.

7

HUMAN BEING

We are human beings. Simple enough sentence. We intuitively know what it means to be human. Don't we? Ask yourself, "What is a human?" What kind of answers do you come up with? What words come to you? Here are some possibilities. We are the thinking animal. We are creatures of the earth. We are mortal beings who seek immortality. We are storytellers. We know isolation, hell, the Voice of Aloneness. Imagination can separate or connect us. There is Another Alone. Isn't there?

I would like to take as our starting point that human beings are mysterious. We don't know all there is to know about life or about being human, and the not knowing can trouble us deeply. It can make us anxious. It can make the world wobble. It can expose us to our isolation. Is that one way to say who we are? We are isolated creatures who hunger to be in relationship.

Or, we are relating creatures who touch misery when we are isolated. But what about the need to be alone? To escape from others, to leave those places where voices and laughter distract us? What about the hunger for solitude? For that aloneness that feeds us? What about our need to be alone with Another Alone? Where we discover that at the heart of our aloneness is relatedness not isolation? And that much of our meeting with fellow human beings leaves us feeling isolated?

THE UNICORN AND THE VIRGIN

I want to try to capture a unicorn. Something that has evaded me my whole life. A unicorn can only be captured by a virgin. Unable to fulfill the normal requirements for virginity and unwilling to be stopped in my quest quite so easily, I am here defining virgin as those places previously unvisited in myself. That is, if I am to catch a unicorn, I have to go where I've never gone before. I have to step into a new place within me.

That is precisely where I'm feeling drawn. I want to go to that place in me where aloneness means relationship. Where Another Alone is or has the possibility of being. To a place of paradox, of mystery, where isolation leads me to you. Because it leads me to me. Where more than myself is waiting in the middle of me.

Human being. That creature who has at his or her middle something greater than himself. Permit yourself to get uncomfortable with this. Like a person containing a skyscraper. Like the person who goes inside and finds a skyscraper to enter into. Like the person who gets small enough—just like Alice in Wonderland—to enter into the small places teeming inside himself.

Or pictured another way, there is a world in there. Maybe this explains why we sometimes feel so full that we can't take anything else in. Though I doubt it. Unless the feeling is caused by a pull to this other world, a need to enter this other place that people have known about and talked about since the beginning of time. Except for those Westerners who believe that the tangible world is the only world. How very much we have ignored!

But it *is* the only world. How about that? Let's walk down that road for a minute. This is the only world. All that goes on inside us is imaginary. We can explain to some people's satisfaction why people fabricate (this time it means to make up, to lie, not to make up, as in to create) stories about our being more than we are, that is, mortal creatures destined to die who have evolved to the degree that we know we're going to die. Cruel evolution.

We are creatures who, in knowing that we're mortal, long to be immortal. Does that make sense? And if it does, what does that tell us? That to be human is to be crazy, to not accept who we are. Human beings, then, are those creatures who, on discovering our mortality, become insane. We begin believing that there is more to us than mortal being. Begin searching frantically for that "more." Name it God, Allah, the Great Spirit, Wotan, Kali, Durga, Shiva, Another Alone. And then claim (if you listen to some) that having experienced God, Allah, the Great Spirit, they *know* that there is another world. They are certain that there is more to life than they previously supposed. They even find that their isolation has been ended.

Two questions. Are these people crazy? And if so, is it advisable to be crazy? Seriously. Andrew Greeley did a survey which found that the group of people who claimed to have had spiritual experiences were the most healthy, most emotionally mature group, according to an oft-used emotional maturity scale. One possible explanation. They *are* crazy and certain kinds of craziness help people to survive and thrive in the midst of mortality. That is, it is a crazy world that confronts its inhabitants with the fact that they are there on a temporary basis, expected to vacate at a moment's notice. And no, we're terribly sorry, we can't find you digs anywhere else because there isn't anywhere else.

Or try this. This is the only world. And we have misunderstood it terribly. This only world is full of dimensions the likes of which Horatio never dreamed. Or if he did have dreams, he forgot or ignored them. Dimensions. What is this? Earlier I said there is another world. Now I'm saying dimensions. The word helps. This can't be the only world if it contains other worlds in it, particularly if the other worlds are inside of us, and are larger than the space they occupy.

But it can be a world of many dimensions of which we occupy one. There. That helps, doesn't it? What we know about the visible universe may also be true within. There are billions of galaxies, each containing billions of stars. The earth is a tiny planet of a minor star of an average galaxy. Now consider this, fellow virgin. Consider that there is an immensity within us that is not unlike the whole universe. Packed neatly in dimensions for storage purposes. What if these dimensions are yours for the viewing? What if there are worlds unimagined where you can learn about life?

This sounds like what many drug gurus suggest. But I don't think we need drugs. What we need is openness and curiosity. Maybe there are some worlds that we're not meant to see. Some dimensions, I mean. Maybe access to these worlds gets us into trouble. Like hell. Like that place of isolation.

Revelation. How about that? Maybe we find ourselves already in places where we're not meant to be. Maybe we aren't meant to be so isolated. Maybe that's what gives the Voice of Aloneness such power. Maybe that's why Another Alone is there in the middle of the isolation, to open it to us. To show us that even at the heart of isolation is the offer of relation.

And revelation. Revelation, my etymological dictionary tells me, comes from the Old and Middle French *revel*, meaning to revolt, and then merrymaking. Revelation in this sense is a revolt against what is. Is-olation, if you'll forgive me. Revelation revolts against isolation and discloses, opens, another dimension, a beyond, and invites us to merrymaking. Weird. And, by the way, Revelator, the Halloween party wasn't such a gas.

The word human comes from *humus*, meaning of the earth. Humus, as we know, is dirt. Rich dirt. A beautiful song by a group named Kansas proclaimed that "all we are is dust in the wind." Troubling, upsetting lyrics. Maybe wrong, too. Maybe we are rich, dirt not dust. Fertile dirt. Or better, fecund dirt. Because fertility requires the planting of a seed. And with that, there goes our virginity.

I'm not just playing word games with you. I'm searching for a unicorn. I'm trying to find my virginal self. Wait. A chill goes up my spine. Isolation. Revelation. Maybe isolation is our virginal place. Where we are untouched. Horribly untouched, as we've seen. Could it be that isolation is fertile ground for the unicorn?

Maybe revelation can only open in isolation. And isolation is purposeful. Can be used to good purpose. Maybe we are meant to be creatures of solitude. Creatures who go off by ourselves so that revelation can come. Maybe then we are to share our revelations that come in our solitude.

But wait a minute. The isolation I've been describing is hell. Am I saying that the universe purposely puts us in hell to show us heaven? Fourth-century theologian Lactantius said much the same thing. Evil is there to show us how good good is. To quote: "God willed this distinction and distance between good and evil so that we might be able to grasp the nature of good by contrasting it with the nature of evil." That angers me. Deeply. It fixes the universe in a way that doesn't feel true to me.

Then how about this? Another Alone, the Revelator as I'm supposing, is everywhere, offering revolt and merrymaking, even in hell. Is there any documentation for such a view?

I think first of the woman in the concentration camp who offered to die for another woman who was terrified. She took the other woman's place in line and died for her. I don't know what happened to the woman who was saved. Odds are that she died, too. But was she changed by this offer? Was this a revelation, a revolt against the isolation of the crowded death camp? Did Another Alone speak through the woman who gave her life? Big questions. We don't know. But we have the story. It was remembered. It touched someone in hell enough to be remembered. Is this a cause for merrymaking? What a revolting idea! But let me dare it. "Yes," I want to cry out. It *is* cause for merrymaking. It shows, though it doesn't prove, that Another Alone is working even in hell. Which is cause for profound merrymaking. And crazy.

This last paragraph gives me pause. You see what I just did with the word revelation? Opened it up just the slightest bit, and found a revolution hiding there. Full of merrymaking. Isn't that a curious thing? Does it surprise you to find revelation so full?

Revelation is often spoken of in quiet tones, as in, "She was given a revelation of God." Or seriously, as in, "That stock is worthless? That's a revelation to me." However, here we're looking at a word that's full of revolution and merrymaking. The sense of revelation that the word suggests to me is, "We've got something of major importance going on here." Take Halloween in my case. First class revelation there, a revolution in my life that has taken me twenty years to understand. Or to begin to understand. Where is the merrymaking, though? What if it's right here? What if we are making merry here in the middle of hell? As in, "That was one hell of a party."

I think we're onto something. That heroic woman in the concentration camp gives us something to make merry about. She shows us that there is something more than isolation in isolation. And not only Another Alone. Something human. That woman stepped into another person's isolation (and out of her own) when she offered to die for her. She caused a small revolution, too. Was remembered and is still being talked about today.

Even more, her act has the power to change us fifty years later. Do you believe that? Are you touched when you imagine a worn-out, skinny woman walking slowly up to a poor, shrieking soul and saying, "I'll die for you"?

Can you let yourself stand in the shrieking woman's shoes? Feel what it's like to be in line to die. Feel the weakness in your knees. Hear the thoughts shouting in your mind. "I'm going to die! I'll never see my family again! It's really happening. They're going to kill me. Put me in that gas chamber, then burn me up in the ovens. What kind of hell is this? What kind of monster God made the world? I'm going to die. No, no! Aieii! What? Who is touching me?

Those soft fingers tapping me. Look at her eyes. So full of something I only vaguely remember. So full of something new. She is
pulling my arm. She is pulling at me. Where are the guards? They
will shoot her for this. She is pulling my arm. Oh God, oh my God,
she's stepping in line for me! What can this mean? I am left to live
another day. Here in hell. Because she heard my shriek. There she
goes, and I, to her death. I go with her. She is going to my death.
Facing my death for me. Gone. What? That little boy is crying. His
mommy is in line, too. I will go to him. What is happening to me?
I will go to him. And hold him."

WHAT ARE WE HUMANS?

Human being. What is human being? Is it a vast dimension of
reality, much of it little explored? Gerard Manley Hopkins says it
this way: "Oh the mind, the mind has mountains; cliffs of fall/
Frightful, sheer, no-man-fathomed." Is human being full of revolution and merrymaking? Does human being bring to the world something it has before lacked? Does it open reality in new ways? Do other
creatures know that they are isolated? Are they? Look in a dog's eyes
sometime. Is the dog isolated? Is the dog connected to you?

I think of the experiments done with heart patients and dogs. The
heart patients who had dogs to pet were less anxious, less overwhelmed by the seriousness of their situation, than those who who
didn't. They were brought out of the terror of isolation by stroking
a dog. Do we want to be as we imagine dogs to be? Relatively
simple, loving, unconscious beings who thrive on love and offer
themselves freely to be petted? Are we too afraid to be petted? Are
others too afraid to pet us, especially if we admit we want to be
petted? Can most of us ask to be petted only when we're sick?
"Mom, rub my back. I don't feel good." How about "Pull me close,
honey. I feel like merrymaking"?

Okay. We human beings get smarter when we're sick. At least we
can ask for what we need more easily. Or, the other person is freer
to love us when we're sick. Because we're not so damn isolated.
When we are sick, we can moan. If we're sick enough. Usually, we
hide those moans, don't we? We are so scared to let our isolated
moaners be seen. They only manage to squeak out when we are too
weak to care what others think.

ANOTHER EXERCISE

Try moaning for a second. Go ahead, let a moan come out of your mouth. Go to another room if you need to. Go into the bathroom and turn on the fan. Just moan. Let yourself feel where the moan starts. Feel it in your throat. In your chest if it reaches down that far. In your belly. Monitor your feelings. Do you feel different when you moan? Do you feel better? Do memories come up of moaning times? Are your moans like revelations, full of packed away meanings?

Isolation. Moaning. Moaning makes us feel better. It is also a sound, a calling out to another. A cry. "Help me, help me! I feel so terrible."

Wild thought next. And maybe the book's going to take a crazy turn, zoom like a tornado into a surprising new direction. Here we go. Moaning is Another Alone speaking in you. Calling out of your isolation in your illness for another. Another Alone is speaking for you. Even while the Voice of Aloneness might be shouting in you, "Will you shut up? Will you stop this noise? Don't you realize that you sound like a fool? And now that damn dog is whining with you. Shut up! Shut up!"

But Another Alone moans. Another wild thought. Your moaning is the sound of God. Is that too much? The Creator, the Omnipotent, All-Knowing One moaning? Your moaning is the sound of God in you. Just as that doomed woman's shriek was God. Horrible thought, isn't it? Messes up the neat world again, with God sitting atop it, turning everything to good.

No. God is in the middle of it turning everything to good. Or at least trying to turn everything to good. Shrieking if necessary. Imagine it with me. In the middle of that woman as she walks to her death, God shrieks. And is heard! This is the importance of the moment. God's shriek was *heard*. And was responded to. God came into being there for a moment. And was remembered, by whatever name we use. God the moaner, the shrieker, dissolved the isolation. In the middle of a concentration camp. Impossibly, wonderfully, horribly true. That woman walked to her death. That other woman was returned to live another day in the killing camp. The good news is not that liberation of the camp happened at that moment. The good news is that God shrieked and was heard.

Let's follow this crazy spin. I was going to write about love next.

But I think I'll write about God instead. You may be thinking, "God *is* love." At least, that's the rumor around town. It's sure tough to believe it sometimes. Here in isolation we need a loud shriek and a gentle hand. Specifics. Not theology in the abstract. As Sargent Friday used to say on the television program "Dragnet," "Just the facts, ma'am. Just the facts." Let's give it a try. One warning: I don't know any more than you do what we'll find. Revolution maybe. Revelation. Merrymaking. Mmmm. Ooooo. Aieii. The moans and shrieks are riding the wind as we walk on. God is speaking.

8

GOD

I am staring at the chapter title. God. I'm going to tell you about God now. I'm going to talk about God. Am I? Do I have anything to say about God? Can I say anything that is at all true? How do we dare speak of God? When we say that God is the source of all things. The Creator. The one who calls us into being. Are we not entering the Holy of Holies when we speak of God? How presumptuous to imagine God to be at the center of us. To be in the middle of hell with us. To be moaning. And shrieking.

Do I offend you when I say God shrieks with that woman in the concentration camp? Is God that caught up with us? And if so, what might that mean?

GOD, THE MOANER AND SHRIEKER

God is moaning and shrieking. God the Creator is moaning and shrieking. What is this moaning and shrieking business? I'm getting caught on the words. Moaning and shrieking. To moan can feel good when I'm sick. To hear another person moan is a different story. It reaches deep into me. Pulls me embarrassingly close to that other. Tells me that person is in pain. Is trying to relieve her pain. Is sounding her inner being into the world. Is sharing her privacy publicly. With me. How am I supposed to react to that invitation into privacy? To that great and painful honor of seeing another's secret places?

And shrieking. What a harsh word. The sound carries its meaning. The sound tears the air around it. Expresses the tear in the other's being. A shriek is an announcement of anguish, an outburst of soul, an invitation into hell.

God in hell. That, too, is a troubling thought. But less troubling, isn't it, than to think of God leaving us deserted in hell? A woman shrieks as she walks to her death. A shriekless God. It doesn't feel good. Doesn't feel right. That God is aloof. Do you want a God who stands idly by while a woman shrieks? Just like we ourselves do so often. Do you want a God who does shriek, who is the shriek, calling out to you? Pressing you into action? In a concentration camp. At the moment of death. When there is nothing for you to do. Nothing at all. Except to give your life. Futilely. Because she is going to die anyway. Maybe tomorrow.

Viktor Frankl, who himself survived the concentration camps, writes in his book *Man's Search for Meaning* of a prisoner who was caught in a nightmare. Frankl was torn by the person's groaning. Should he wake the person up from the nightmare? Into what? An even greater nightmare.

I am struggling here. We move through hell asking questions of God. Craziness. Hearing God crying in another's moaning. Looniness. I'm feeling like I can't do this. Like I can't get at God here. Like maybe I'm way off the mark. How does that feel? What are you answering me? "It's about time"? Or, "Don't give up. Listen again to the moan. Don't tell me you've opened me up to my own moaning only to back away."

That helps. It brings me back. I was thinking, not listening to the moaning and shrieking. Avoiding the moaning and shrieking by trying to figure it out. When someone moans or shrieks, you can't figure it out. You can only respond to it.

Does that tell us something about God? Does God want us to respond to the hell-trapped person rather than to think about him? Maybe God isn't a moral theologian. Maybe God is a person. Shocking? Does it shock you to think of God as a person? Or is God obviously a person to you?

I want to erase all this and start over. I don't think I'm going to because there is value in seeing a person struggle with God. And hope when, if, the person suddenly finds a way to open to God. Will I succeed? That is the hell of it, isn't it? We don't know. I may have come this far only to fail. That crazy spin I mentioned in the last chapter may carom me into a dead end. That makes me sad. To be able to share hell, but not to share God.

TALKING WITH GOD

Shall I do an audacious thing? Watch. I've no idea if this will work either.

"God, have you anything to say?"

Silence. I look at my watch. It's 4:40 A.M. Middle of the night. Good God time.

Silence. Maybe hell is the condition of being without God.

"God, have you anything to say?"

I see that woman walking into the gas chamber for another. That's all. Is that God's answer? And if it is?

"Is it, God? Have you anything else to say?"

I see that little boy weeping as his mother walks to her death.

To be honest, I feel like swearing, hell creature that I am. I feel like yelling. But what? My heart races. Something is happening. God? God in my yell? In my desire to yell? If I really do yell, I'll wake my family. Scare the hell out of them, too. Imagine that. Yelling in the middle of the night.

"What's wrong, dear?" my wife would ask. "I was just thinking about God and hell and concentration camps. I needed to yell."

But I'm not yelling. Where does that yelling that I'm not yelling go? Does it find its way into my soul? Does it feed the Voice of Aloneness? Does it serve the negativity? Does it lead me deeper into hell? Is it God wanting to yell in me?

"Is it, God?"

I am letting myself moan. It's quiet. No one else is awake. I'm not bothering anyone. Except myself. I'm entering my moan. Closing my eyes. Searching the moan. Feeling two things.

"This is nuts. Erase the whole thing. Press the delete button."

You recognize the Voice of Aloneness. The other feeling. Just moan. Get up from the computer. Go sit on the couch and moan. I'm going now. I'll be back in a minute. It's now 4:53 A.M.

I took several minutes. It's now 5:04. First, I moaned and felt the tiredness of my body. From getting up so early to write about God. Then a sense of relaxation. Moaning invited me into my tiredness. Then I worried about the chapter and about God. Am I way off the mark? Words came to me. That were spoken to me yesterday by a woman as she left my office. "God is crazy, wild, and sneaky." That's a quote. I wrote it down on a piece of paper immediately after she left. Words of God.

THE CRAZY, WILD, SNEAKY GOD

How does that grab you? "God is crazy, wild, and sneaky." What does she mean by it? Here is a person who has struggled all her life with God. Her father left the family when she was a small child. She was sent to live with her uncle, who sexually abused her for several years, until she graduated from high school and could leave. Her life is a story of broken relationships, of being hurt by men, and not trusting women. Of isolation. And self-hatred. Of wanting to destroy her sexuality and her person. Of fearing that God, who knew all about her, would condemn her to hell forever. Where she already was.

Something crazy, wild, and sneaky has been happening to her. She is opening herself to herself. She is admitting that she is full of desire. Of sexual desire. Of desire to be in human relationship. Even after the many disasters in her life. Of desire to be with God. And torn. Because she wants the human and fears that if she finds God she will lose the human. For God will preempt or overwhelm her need for the human. Will take the human away.

"Why?" I have asked her again and again. "Why would God take away the human?"

"Because that's the way God is."

She doesn't fully believe that. "God is crazy, wild, and sneaky." She is looking into the middle of her desire for the human and finding God. Right there, in the middle of her desire. In the wish to be touched by a man. Lovingly, not abusively. And seeing it as possible. It sounds like God's moaning to me. Once again, God is hanging out where her truth is. In her urgent desire.

Can you open to your own urgent desire? Do you have an urgent desire? Does this desire embarrass you, make you feel shy? Do you long to be touched lovingly, petted? In a way that feels forbidden or impossible? Open that up. Find your feeling there. Face your feeling. Imagine that God is in that feeling. Do you want to hide? To apologize to God. For being a sexual being. Even though you want to whisper under your breath, "You're the one who made me sexual." And of course, God hears that almost whisper.

A story of transformation. But first, a warning. I don't believe you can talk truly about God without being graphic. To say "I love God" and to leave it there says nothing to me. And it doesn't reach very deep into you. In fact, it may be a cop-out. I'm suggesting that

God is where the action is. Not sitting in the sky waiting for you to come home. *If* you get your act together. Otherwise, you're going to end up in hell. Get stuck reading this book. Where the author will suggest God is right in the middle of your suffering, because, as my friend says, "God is crazy, wild, and sneaky." It would be just like a sneaky God to hang out in hell.

A story of transformation. That has to do with masturbation. For years this woman masturbated, not to find pleasure, but in an attempt to rub out her sexuality. She tried to kill her femininity. And failed. Thank crazy, wild, sneaky God. And now she is just beginning to love her body, to appreciate her femininity.

Am I claiming that God approves of masturbation? That God is in the middle of this? Of course I am. I see crazy, wild, sneaky God there. I see a God who isn't caught up in rules of propriety. Who is a lover. Who wants this woman to love herself. This means rediscovering her desire. Masturbation has been one part of her healing. Of her exclamation about the crazy, wild, sneaky God. Has gotten her attention that she is an embodied woman who longs for God and for human relationship.

GOD AND THE PERSONAL

Something happens when we enter the personal. Did the chapter come alive when I brought forth this woman's story? Was it going nowhere until I found the personal? It was going nowhere for me. What does this tell us? That we need the personal to find the depth of God. That God isn't an idea or a formulation, but a cry in, from, and for the isolated person. A cry to another. Here the plot thickens. The mystery opens. Because God is about relationship. Is about human being. Is about the transformation of individuals and the world.

Just a few pages back, God was moaning. Now I'm claiming to know what God intends for the world. Where is our depression in all this?

The temptation is great to pronounce the meaning of the world. That's not the point right now, is it? Is it? Let's return to depression. To isolation. It is depressing to be isolated. To be so caught in our *is* that we can't imagine any other possibility. And if our "is" is hellish, depression makes good sense. The Voice of Aloneness is

talking true. It is better to rub out our sexuality, along with everything else.

Which is hell.

Which is where we are.

Which is where moaning, shrieking, wild, crazy, sneaky God is.
Who wants, so I believe, hell not to be ultimate. Who is willing to
be a bellowing fool if that can bring us to deeper, more fulfilling life.
If that can make isolation so unbearable that we will break from it
out of sheer desperation.

God is a desperate-maker. When in hell, shriek, bellow, moan.
That is the message I hear. You just might be heard by another
human being. And you might not. Which is exactly what we fear
because we've experienced not being heard so many times before.
And it is terrible. It pushes us even deeper into isolation.

Where God keeps moaning. As though God doesn't give up.
Even in the killing camp. At the last possible moment. Something
big happened when one woman took another's place to die. I can't
shake that image. It would be just like a crazy, wild, sneaky God to
grab me that way. To help me say something about who this God is.

I can't help myself. I've got to pronounce. Do with it what you
need to. Toss it out as garbage. Hold onto it for dear life. Whatever.
I hope it speaks to you.

Pronouncement. The God who is shrieking and moaning and all
the other things I'm suggesting is, I believe, concerned with making
relationship. Between people. Between people and God. Between
the God in one person and the God in another person. Between
sexes, races, and countries. Between us and the animals. Because—
audacious pronouncement—God's goal is relationship. True relationship frees people from isolation. Opens them to revelation.

Relationship is revolutionary. Relationship converts us. Conversion, from the word *metanoia*, means to turn around. I can leap
quickly to revolving, then to revolution. And what is the revolution, the revelation, the merrymaking invitation? It is a call to
everyone—not just to the consciously depressed and isolated
ones—to be involved in making the cosmos, to help create the
world. The world wasn't created in seven days. It is still being
created. It is still an open story.

CONVERSATIONAL CONVERSION

I have an idea that I've toyed with for about a year. I call it conversational conversion. Notice the relationship between the two words. Conversing and conversion. I play with the words. Does conversion, turning around, revolution, revelation, occur in conversation? Is the experience of conversion, of turning around, a measure that true conversation has happened? Have I not conversed with you if I am not changed? Isn't that the main purpose of conversation? To give some kind of important information to the other? Whether it be about the weather, the children, or one's soul?

When we are isolated, conversation can be terribly difficult. When our isolation comes from a sense of worthlessness, how can we dare to converse with anyone? How can we share what we fear will change the other's attitude toward us? Is this why God speaks in moans? Sneaks out of us through our sounds? So that necessary conversation has a chance to happen? Moaning, then, would be a wish to converse. From the very core of ourselves. And under protest. I don't want to cry out my misery.

How do you respond to another's groan? Do you run from it? Or try to fix it? "There, there, dear, it isn't so bad." And if that moan is God, Another Alone speaking on behalf of an isolated soul? What then? Will you listen differently, more carefully, more nervously now? Will you open to that moan even if it is coming from your own mouth?

I want to suggest that your isolation isn't healed by being saved by another, but instead by seeing that your isolation touches another and changes her or him. Because this tells you that you are there. In conversation with another. *Quod agit existit.* "That which acts exists." By changing another, you discover your own existence. You enter into conversation with another struggling human being.

But. Without the moaning, without God's voice, conversation doesn't lead to conversion when you are in hell. Only that magic element, heard as moans and sighs, can change us, can turn us around, can get us revolving toward revelation and merrymaking. Now to that magic element.

9

LOVE

All sorts of thoughts pass through my mind as I try to start this chapter. Words from songs come. "Love is a wonderful thing." "Love hurts." "Only love can break a heart, only love can mend it again." "She loves you, yeah, yeah, yeah."

St. Paul speaks: "Love bears all things."

I remember a fact: A recent widow or widower is significantly more likely to die in the year after her or his loved one dies.

And this desire: To speak passionately about love. How else? For love is a passionate thing. Can we speak *about* love? Or can we only speak as lovers do, by being *in* love?

But there is no love in hell's isolation. Except for moans.

I want us to let go in this chapter. I want us to open ourselves to passionate love. Can we loosen our minds so that God's moaning enters us and changes us? Can we forget to think about this for just a little while? Can we just open to the mystery of love, letting it touch us and teach us?

THE FIRE OF HELL AND HEAVEN

How can love speak to us in hell? How can we find love residing in isolation? It sounds like a contradiction in terms. Love, by definition, is relational. Let's start where we are. We now know not to drag a person from isolation as from a burning fire. Rather, we are to walk into the flames and sit there together. Even if it burns the hell out of us. That's a curious turn of phrase, isn't it? Maybe we need to have hell burned out of us rather than to get out of hell. Moaning, then, makes a certain kind of sense.

Let's come back again to God, the moaner. Can we open that a little more? We moan when we are feeling pain, don't we? Moaning means pain, is the expression of it. We admit our pain when we moan. We make ourselves vulnerable to the world. We moan to communicate. How dreadful, then, to moan when there is no one to hear us. When we are isolated. If God is moaning *there*. What? What is God doing? Isn't the timing all wrong? Or is God crying shamelessly into the world for us, begging for someone, anyone, to hear our pain? Trying to tear us open to our isolation so we will desperately seek others? Forcing us to free ourselves from the dishonesty of the shielded isolation?

I resent that last question. Job scratching his boils is being dishonest? Admitting that we find ourselves dragging our way through hell isn't dishonest. It's not honesty we're having trouble with. It's the sound of isolation. It's the pain of isolation speaking the truth of where we are. Making us desperate, like panicky horses when the barn is on fire.

There's the fire again.

I think of the following words from Buddha's Fire Sermon: "All things, O priests, are on fire . . . the eye, O priests, is on fire; . . . the ear is on fire; sounds are on fire; . . . the nose is on fire; the tongue is on fire; things tangible are on fire; . . . the mind is on fire; ideas are on fire".

Buddha's solution to the fire is to conceive an aversion to the eye, the ear, to sounds, and to all things in the world. In so conceiving, we become divested of our passion, freed of suffering and rebirth, and are no longer caught in this world.

It's a good solution. But I find myself walking the other way. *Into* the fire. Though on this much we agree: There's a fire blazing.

There's a fire blazing. Life, Buddha calls it. A fire we're calling hell, when it burns in the place of isolation. My mind leaps to a story about St. Catherine of Genoa in which she takes a hardened sinner directly from hell to heaven. (Dante, remember, took the long way.) On his arrival in heaven, the man cries these words: "No suffering in Hell could match the torture of being drowned in love when everything within me is corrupt."

I want to struggle with this man's torture. For him, heaven is too much, too real, too overwhelming, to be borne. Hell offers him some kind of relief in its isolation. Because the relatedness of heaven is impossible for him, and for us, all at once. As though the isolation of hell is somehow necessary first. Purifying. Bringing us to the unbearable nothing, causing God to moan, because perhaps finally in our loneliness, we are ready to take our first steps toward true relating.

Why do these words of e.e. cummings come to me now? "love is less always than to win/less never than alive/less bigger than the least begin/less littler than forgive."

Am I making sense? Does cummings speak now precisely because I don't understand, to put me in my lack of understanding, to free me to be isolated enough to moan? Then I am moaning right now, wanting you to hear me. Wanting you to join me in my isolation. And then?

I'll struggle to tell you what I know of love in hell. My first inclination is to leave the next six pages empty. That would be symbolic and a kind of honesty. But not helpful to you. Unless you speak the language of nothingness.

Or, I can just let myself open. Let myself moan. Let myself dare to believe that that moaning is God, my Virgil, groaning directions how to make my way, our way, to that other too hot place, heaven, at the top of that too high hill, that hell of a hill, which, if Catherine speaks true, if her sinner speaks true, *is* harder than hell to be in. So the moaner comes to us. To moan of the pain of hell and the fear of heaven.

Let us moan.

PASSION

Love is the passion of our being. The singing in our souls. The urge to connect, to be, to become, to come alive. Love calls. (I don't know what I'm talking about. I'm moaning.) Love is the other. The beautiful one. The sexy one. The belly and below-the-belly urge to couple, to one, to be a wonderful couple.

"One's not half two. It's two are halves of one" says e. e. cummings in his unmistakable way.

There is a Hebrew word for love, *ahavah*, which does not soar above the body, but connects the body and the soul, sees the sacred in the midst of the profane.

There is eros. You know eros. Feel it in your belly now, in your memory, if you can. Eros draws us to another like a strong magnet, like the flame that calls the moth, then scorches it. Eros is like that, isn't it? The Greeks know three types of eros. *Anteros* is the drawing love of the lover to the beloved. *Himeros* is the response of the beloved. And then there is *pothos. Pothos* is insatiable longing. Longing which can't be satisfied. Ever. Because by definition it is insatiable. That's the is that it is. That is the is of isolation too, isn't it? Unless we've given up and become depressed. Unless we have ceased squealing and squeaking. But even there, a moan. A cry of soul, in the soul, even when there's no you left to cry it. What else can that moan be but God, Other, the Silly Something Else that can't read the writing on the wall? That bellyaches for you insatiably.

What? What is this? A suggestion that God is pothotic? Is full of insatiable longing for you? Maybe you respond with a "Yikes, get me out of here!" Like that guy Catherine of Genoa transported straight to heaven.

Except if moans be God, God comes to you. God is insatiable. God is so full of desire for you—and I mean the sexy, more than sexy kind—that hell is no barrier for God. Nor is isolation.

Wow. I'm not saying I believe this, mind you. But the insatiability of *God*? If I don't think about it, it explains the whole universe, with its billions of galaxies, with its platypi (platypuses?), and all the other stuff that doesn't seem to help me get my thing done. A universe which travels at thousands and thousands of thousands of miles per hour through the vast darkness. The whole of it is a burst of insatiability from God, for me, for you. It could swell a person's head, pop it right open, in fact, if taken seriously, if taken playfully.

But we don't take it seriously or playfully. We're sane enough to see the nonsense of it. That God could be so wild about me, about you, to spin this great universe into being. And more to the point— "less bigger than the least begin"—and greater than any universe, to come to hell for me, to make a noisy fool of *Herself. Himself? Itself?* Better, to make a noisy fool of *Ourself.* I mean, it's my belly that's sending the noisy message through my vocal cords to your ears. Which, be reminded, are on fire!

Are you with me? And if you are, where in the hell are you? Do you feel the wow of the wildness of the crazy, sneaky, moaning God, who insatiably seeks you, tugs at you, humiliates Ourself out of need for you? What if the Creator, the moaner, created you out of desperate need? For *you?* Another wild question, a moan finding words, comes to me. What if your depression is related to your knowing, somehow, that you are desperately, insatiably, pothotically needed by God, so that God can be whole? Several tons of theological writing have answered that question, I suspect. God doesn't *need* you. God gives you life as a free gift.

Can I answer that from my vantage point in hell? If this isolation is a free gift, where is the return counter? Buddha speaks again, inside me. Fire, the eyes, the tongue, the mind, fire. Life itself, fire. I'm burning up here and you're telling me, trying to convince me that my isolation *isn't*. And may I add that you are proving what you are trying to disprove? Horribly, you may be right. Maybe the whole thing is a blessed gift, and I'm just plain stupid. It could be so. Makes for a short book, though. And a depressing one, too.

> DEPRESSION. Chapter One.
>   You are depressed. You have no reason to be depressed because God gives you life freely. The End.

Indeed. The end. But if God needs me, and you, and the silly platypus, and makes us out of need—*our* need I want to say, though I don't yet come close to knowing why—then there's hope, a possibility of *beginning*. Which is the proposal presently on the table.

Once again, wow. This moaning, sneaky God is in this for personal reasons. Another leap. God's need explains romantic passion. If you don't think too hard about it. Romantic passion is the longing for Ourself, beyond myself, that little moaning critter who is isolated in hell and shooting off his mouth to beat the band, maybe because he can't bear the silence, or maybe because (wow) God needs him.

A BRIEF DIALOGUE WITH THE
VOICE OF ALONENESS

The Voice of Aloneness now asks, "What kind of nonsense is all this?"

I answer, "Exciting nonsense, Al. Do you mind if I call you Al?"

VOICE: *"You're making a fool of yourself."*

ME: *"A fool who can dance for a bit. Instead of sitting deadly*

*by, watching my life end, and end, and end. What if, Al, I throw
in a little philosophy to make it slightly more respectable?"*

VOICE: "You're going to anyway."

*ME: "Right. Plato said that love is a form of divine madness.
Along with creativity, prophecy, and healing."*

VOICE: "I never liked Plato very much."

*ME: "No wonder, Al. You don't like Plato because you have no
wonder."*

DIVINE MADNESS IN HELL

How is love a kind of divine madness? Certainly the madness part
of it is easy for most of us to understand. It is this madness of love
that has chased many of us into isolation. But divine? What could
that mean? Is love a creative madness, a healing madness, a pro-
phetic one?

Oh yes, yes, yes, I dare to say. Yes. But then I feel hell's dullness
again pulling at me. Negating me. Tugging at me and the whole
universe like an infinite black hole, drawing me, us, and the blessed
platypi toward nothingness, beyond isolation. Where the fire has
gone out.

The yes has gone. The oh stretches into oooooo again, moans.
We know what that means, or what I claim it means, what I want it
to mean. I'm being pothotically honest here, showing my pothos
honestly, like a wild, hungry lover. Oooooo means that God is
speaking. Are you listening? Have you been listening to my (our)
moaning? What do you make of it, of this madness? Divine?
Cuckoo?

I call myself a wild, hungry lover, image myself thus, use a
metaphor to express, to press-out of me, that fire inside. What is
this? How are you reacting to my wooing? To my come on? To my
asking you to dance with me? To have intercourse? Whatever the
word means to you here, consider that intercourse comes from the
Old and Middle French *entrecors*, meaning, if I understand my
dictionary, exchange. Intercourse is any kind of exchange. Conversation is a kind of intercourse. Sexual intercourse is a particular
kind of exchange, of conversation. And the exchange sadly fails
there as often as it does with words.

Wait. Who is the lover here? Who is the moaner here? God is.

That's the suggestion. Well, I am too. That's the feeling. Another wild leap. Maybe we are instruments of God for each other. But are we trumpets or scalpels? Do we get to dance or have to submit to surgery?

What about you? What about your moaning and your wildness? What about your hunger? W. H. Auden writes: "For the error bred in the bone/Of each woman and each man/Craves what it cannot have/not universal love/But to be loved alone."

Pothos. Craving what you cannot have. Is this true? Can you live with this truth? Can you open yourself to it? The utter insatiability of life that makes you want anything, even death, in its stead?

Except—can you accept this?—there is that moaning in the middle of you, in the middle of hell, that is being sucked by the nothing toward the nothing. The moan. Will you take some time now and be divinely mad? Squeeze words from the moans in you? Make a wild, crazy fool of yourself? Like God who sits in hell inside you. For the craziness, trust me, is incarnation, is life, is a reverse spin on nothingness, more powerful than the magnetic pull of the black hole, and smaller than a platypus, though "less littler than forgive".

10

INCARNATION

The New Lexicon Webster's Dictionary defines incarnate as
"embodied, especially in human flesh, [as in] *the incarnate God,
[and] he is greed incarnate.*" Christianity, of course, is based on the
first definition. Jesus is believed by Christians to be the embodiment
of God. Pagans, too, celebrate rituals and make sacrifice to the
fertility gods and goddesses who embody themselves in the harvest.

THE PROBLEM WITH MATERIALISM

The word is full of assumptions. To incarnate is to embody. What is
embodied? Who is doing the embodying? And from where? To
materialists, to our brethren of the last couple hundred years, this is
nonsense. There is nowhere that isn't physical. Physical is the basic
stuff. Incarnation is thus a word that carries the nonsense and
superstition of old. That's all.

But that doesn't help us hellians, does it? Again we have the
notion that what we feel, our depression and despair, and love too,
don't come from anywhere. We're back to the craziness explanation
again. Don't worry, folks. Only give up any notion of hell and
you'll be out of it.

That's right. We'll be out of it. But not out of hell. Out of the
wholly physical universe, the universe that is wholly physical, that
has no other stuff but physical stuff. But listen to the words of
physicist, Erwin Schrodinger: "[T]he scientific picture of the real
world around me is very deficient. It gives a lot of factual information, puts all our experience in a magnificently consistent order, but
it is ghastly silent about all and sundry that is really near to our
heart, . . . [I]t knows nothing of beautiful and ugly, good or bad,

God and eternity. Science sometimes pretends to answer questions in these domains, but the answers are very often so silly that we are not inclined to take them very seriously."

Exactly. To us in hell, the notion of a purely physical world is silliness. Isn't it? Or else, we're crazy. But to feel so bad and to be crazy to boot is just too much. So I ran to a great physicist, a student of the physical, who agreed. Einstein said much the same thing. Along with many others. But that's not our point now. Something resonates with Schrodinger's notion of silliness, which frees us to be somewhere real. Hell.

INCARNATING IN HELL

So once again we are free to be in hell. And to ponder incarnation. Incarnate derives from the Latin *incarnatus, incarnare*, which means "to invest with flesh." We come back to those questions. Who is the investor? And where is this investor hiding? A first answer for many would be God. God is the investor. God is the one who invests with flesh whatever stuff it is that gets invested. Material reality comes into being by God's agency; God is the *agit*-ator. Agitate comes from the Latin *agitare*, meaning "to set moving." God thus agitated the world into being, set it moving. Why? A few pages ago, I suggested that God needs us desperately, pothotically, insatiably. If this is so, can agitation be far behind?

So to say that God is the investor, the embodier of the world, is a good answer. A pretty good answer. An answer anyway. A hell of an answer. God embodies. Moans. Calls into existence. Is still calling into existence with moans and shrieks. Is calling us into existence and out of isolation. Which to us folks trapped in hell feels like the only existence. And perhaps is *only* existence. In which case existence isn't so hot. Let me rephrase that. Isn't so wonderful.

What if there are other investors? What if the Voice of Aloneness is one of the investors? What if the Voice of Aloneness fills the world with nothingness? Kind of crazy, isn't it? Which is just how it feels to us. What if the Voice of Aloneness is spewing, and shrieking, and moaning nothingness into the world, and we depressed ones are splattered by the spewing and overwhelmed by the shrieking and moaning so that we can hear nothing else? Incarnating the nothing. Terrifying. It would be wonderful if we could just disappear the nothing with a denial of it. That, in fact, is what we try to do. But it doesn't work. Rather, it seems to put us in the employ of the nothing. For as long as we are depressed and isolated, aren't we working for the nothing, bringing nothing into the world, decarnating, if I may make up a word?

No. Hurts. That line of thought is the stuff of depression, creates it. Unless what I've suggested before is true. Unless Another Alone (that we're calling God now) is there in the middle of the nothingness. Creation *ex nihilo* as it used to be called. Creation from nothing. So we go to the middlest middle of the nothing—why there doth the investor hide?—and God is creating to beat the band, or suggesting the music to the band. Incarnating.

What about us? Are we incarnating? What are we embodying, investing with flesh? Are our actions agitating reality in a particular way? Are we agitating for the nothing, or for Another Alone?

Am I helping you with my suggestion that you have some responsibility for the agitation of life? Or am I agitating you? Maybe you want to yell at me something like, "I can't take the blame for this, too."

I agree. You shouldn't take the blame. You aren't to blame. We're caught in the middle of a hellish conversation. I believe that you can do something, even though you are helpless. Even though it's hopeless, or seems so, unless Another Alone gets into the agitating here, which is precisely my suggestion and hope.

We're counting on Another Alone, aren't we? It's a real all-or-nothing situation here. Truly. That moaning, shrieking pothotic lover. Does it make you nervous to have such a needy being agitating for you?

DEPRESSION AND THE BODY

I want to make a wild suggestion. If the Voice of Aloneness and Another Alone both incarnate, if their strategies and goals seem radically different, if they both embody, wouldn't we expect them to be involved with our body-beings? How else could it be? They would do their embodying elsewhere? Depression is felt in the body. It is the body that informs us that we are depressed. We feel the lethargy and lack of energy, the hopelessness and the lifelessness in our bodies. Or the rush of anxiety and despair, the agitation and danger, accompanied by a feeling that we can do nothing about it. Creature anxiety, as Karen Horney called it. The sense that we live in a hopeless and hostile world and there is nothing we can do about it. Which in itself can bring about the first condition: depression, lethargy, lack of energy. How could it not to an aware, honest person? Maybe your depression is a measure of your integrity, of your openness to truth. But not only. It also shows how caught you are by the Voice of Aloneness who is spewing nothingness.

Clinical depression is diagnosed by similar symptoms. Lethargy, despair, lack of hope, changes in appetite and sleep habits, lack of sexual desire, thoughts of suicide. None of this is surprising. Isn't this just how a person would react to isolation and loneliness? Are we seeing the agitation of the Voice of Aloneness in depression, making as nothing the person's life? And the agitation of Another Alone who is moaning and crying out?

I'm trying to get to the subject of antidepressant medications here, but I'm having a little trouble. What I'm thinking is this. So far as we understand it, antidepressants work in the brain by changing the balance of certain brain chemicals, called neurotransmitters. After taking these medicines for a time, some people find relief from the above symptoms. Their appetites return. They are able to sleep better. Their moods improve. They feel sexual desire again. They think less of suicide.

What does this mean? Is depression just a biochemical thing? I don't think so. With human beings, nothing is ever just a bio-chemical thing. There is more going on than biochemistry. But biochemistry *is* going on. Finally, I've gotten to my wild suggestion. Could it be that the nothing acts, agitates, embodies itself in the chemistry of human beings? Bringing with it the clear and profound experience of itself, of isolation and hopelessness? Could it be—it sounds like insanity to materialists—that medications can serve Another Alone? By bringing the embodied, chemical situation back into balance?

Let's imagine that this is the case. What then? For me, it puts medication in its proper category. The medicine doesn't answer our questions. Doesn't solve the riddles of existence. And hopefully, doesn't stop us asking our questions. Imaginal psychologist James Hillman is concerned that drugs can be used to abort transforma-tion. He writes; "One could expect Job's friends or the companions of Jesus in Gethsemane today to step forward with a tranquilizer."

That is, to avoid the profound questions that one's life presents. I agree with him. I find frustrating reductionistic doctors who say when depression ends, "There you see? It was only a chemical imbalance." *Only?* No. There was presumably a chemical imbalance that the medications corrected, by agitating for Another Alone.

QUESTIONS OF MEANING

The person relieved of these symptoms is usually grateful. But if her questions remain, she must agitate about them with renewed vigor. The incarnate manifestations of the Voice of Aloneness have been lessened, so to say. It is now possible to look at the questions nakedly, to open to other possibilities and images.

Need I remind you that the naked questions are just as difficult? We are still creatures who die. We still seek meaning. We still long to understand our place in the world. Is it as isolated beings? Arriving alone and departing alone? Is it as related beings who can grow in hope and love? The Voice of Aloneness and Another Alone are, in fact, two role models for us. The Voice of Aloneness affirms the nothing, the isolation, thus driving us further into it. Another Alone moans, gets our attention, begs us to get the attention of others, longs for us to be connected. For our benefit. For the benefit of the other. And also, needy being that God is here proposed to be, for the benefit of Another Alone.

When I give lectures or lead workshops on depression, I meet many people who agree that antidepressant medication has helped them to struggle more creatively with the questions of life. Often, they mention that some people in their churches or prayer groups challenge their taking of medication, saying that it demonstrates their lack of faith. This kind of talk gets my hackles up, gets me growling. "So what?" I want to yell at these absent people, who don't need to come to workshops on depression. "What kind of ignorant response is that to a depressed person who is feeling better? Why aren't you taking his hand and swinging him around in a circle and shouting 'Hooray'?" Do you see what happens in situations like that? The threat of isolation is once again cast upon the person who has been rejoicing, making him wonder, "What the hell did I do now?" And you can guess what else happens, can't you? The person begins to hold back the good news. To fall silent for fear of being rejected. Which encourages isolation. Which . . . well, by now you can fill in the rest.

INCARNATION CONTINUES

Incarnation, as I'm using the word, isn't a onetime event in history. It's happening all the time. Every time we open our mouths, or close them, we are incarnating. Every gesture we make incarnates love, or indifference, or disdain. We are making the world. We are enfleshing something every moment, even if that something is the nothing.

Do you see that the nothing is something? *Quod agit existit*. It acts. It manifests. It uses you and me. It gives a kind of life. It creates hell. Which is the nothing that is. Nothing with consciousness. Brings us to that place where our questions become clear. A question is coming now that I want to avoid. That is implied in Mephistopheles' musings about forever serving the good.

Is the nothing necessary? Translated for depressed and anxious folks, is the nothing only nothing or does it carry in it the seed of possibilities other than itself? I'm afraid we can't avoid becoming philosophers. What is the nature of the nothing? Bear with me. I'm struggling with something new, or nothing new, or a new nothing here. What is the nature of the nothing? Is its nothingness dependent on nothing else? Is it nothing as itself, in itself, of its very nature? Or is it that which is not yet called into being? Is it, in fact, a black hole that tugs at the something in desperation, that sucks at it, not to destroy it, but rather in an attempt to pull itself into being? Is nothing longing to be?

My mind goes to Madeleine L'Engle's wonderful novel about confronting evil, *A Wind In The Door*. Meg, the teenage main character, is attempting to save her brother, Charles Wallace, from an illness caused by the echthroi. He is about to be sucked into the nothing as though he had never existed. Meg, instructed by Prokinoskes the angel, puts her arms around the echthroi who are "spreading their gaping, tearing nothingness across creation. 'Size doesn't matter,'" she is told. "'You can hold them all, Charles and Calvin and Mr. Jenkins and the burning sphere of the newborn star.'" Meg cries out, "I hold you! I love you, I Name you. I Name you, Echthroi. You are not nothing. You are." And moments later,

"Echthroi! You are Named! My arms surround you. You are no longer nothing. You are. You are filled. You are me. You are Meg."

I am overwhelmed by that passage. Meg calls the nothing into being and at that moment in the story, she finds her arms around Charles Wallace. He is going to live.

Do you see how much more powerfully image can convey the nothing than abstract questions can? The questions are good, are important, are vitally necessary. Images are answers to those questions. Images are being, are moans and sighs, are possibilities beyond the nothing for the nothing to be. Creation *ex nihilo*. From nothing. Perhaps that's the game we are in. We are to create from the nothing, to call the nothing into being. And if we don't? The nothing does its nothing thing. It nothings.

There is a lot at stake here. Are we up to it? Might hell seem a little bit comfortable now? We're to call the nothing to be? There's wildness, craziness, probably sneakiness here, too. "To be or not to be," Hamlet's question. That's a good question. That just got biggened for me. Made bigger. To be or not to be affects not only myself, but the whole world.

I'm thinking now Michael Ende's book *The Neverending Story*, in which the Nothing is overtaking the world. In the book, it is the child who is reading it who has the power to call the world back into existence. Daunting stuff. Are we up to it? And what is it? What would we have to do to stop this Nothing? Embrace it in our arms, love it, name it, see that it is in us, is us?

Ow, ow, ow. That's too much. I can't do it. I'm having enough trouble just getting by. And who am I kidding? Getting by? Hah! Rather, I'm trudging through hell, that strange place where God is moaning.

What about *that*? Are you following me into the wildness? Is God crying out to us, to you, for help? Like Peter Pan to the audience when Tinkerbell is sick and dying? Are we to applaud, to believe that something can be? That something is trying to be? That the nothing not embraced is not only nothing, but full of groaning potential? That all of that being so, or assumed to be so, still has me as little old me, who doesn't see, can't begin to imagine, that my little part in it, makes or unmakes the world?

But. I must confess something is making sense. Something is stirring in me that says, "Yes! To be! To invite the not to be to be!" But how? How can I, and you, little images of God as I was taught in childhood, do anything? Bear with me on this. Because I have an answer. My answer is that I have no idea. I don't know how to do it. I don't know what comes next. I'm going to leave my computer in just a moment, not knowing where or if I'll be able to take the next step. If there is a next step. Or where the next step leads, whether off a precipice (to be is not to be!) or into the promised land.

And you? Where are you with this incarnational business? Does it make any sense? And even if no, does it enliven you? Stir something in you? Is there a little light shining, that threatens to go out, to die? Can you clap your hands together? Can you wish for it not to die?

I have to stop for now. So that I can clap with you. May we cause a great ruckus in the middle of the nothing.

I turn toward Another Alone. Bow my head respectfully. Let the maestro begin!

11

EX NIHILO

What will the maestro play? Some unknown music no doubt. It is a curious thing to have no idea what I'm going to write in this chapter. To admit that I don't know what I'm doing. To catch myself in the very act. What will I do? What is to be?

Let's start with some naked imagery. What is your mind doing with that sentence? What is nakedness suggesting to you? Actually, the naked image I was thinking of is hell. Is where we are. That one image changes what naked might mean, doesn't it?

Hell. *Ex nihilo*. *Nihilo* brings to mind annihilate. To bring to nothing. *Ex*nihilate. I've just made up a word. May this be an exnihilating experience for us.

SYMPHONY

Another image. The maestro. The conductor occupies a strange position here. Sits or stands in the middle of me, moaning. The moaning conductor. Picture an orchestra tuning up before a symphony. All the curious sounds blending into a cacophony—which comes from the Greek *kakophonia* meaning bad sound—into a squeaking, shrieking noise. Each player, each instrument, trying to get ready for the symphony.

We are the players in the orchestra. Many of us don't know the music for tonight. Or how to tune our instruments. That makes for an interesting image, doesn't it? A symphony, led by a moaning conductor, full of musicians who know neither the music nor their assigned instruments. What kind of sound will the maestro produce?

I notice a feeling of dread. What is going to happen here? What am I doing?

I'm trying to suggest how to be in the nothing. How to open to Another Alone in hell. How to take an attitude of openness and wait for the music to begin. It's hard to do this. Hard to trust. And also a real opportunity. A chance to do the real thing right now.

The Voice of Aloneness interrupts: "You're so full of it."

Of what? Of the nothing? Of the urge for something? I *am* full of it. But what is it?

The Voice doesn't answer. It chooses not to speak further. A greater silence comes. As though the instruments are all tuned, but we still don't know what music to play.

DIALOGUE WITH THE MAESTRO

ME: Another Alone, it is time for you to speak.

ANOTHER ALONE: Open.

ME: I don't want to open. I do. After all, this is hell and being open isn't the happiest of feelings here.

ANOTHER ALONE: It's not that kind of symphony. Open. It is a symphony from the silence. It is played with the ears. Tune your ears to hear the borning symphony.

ME: I picture Mozart writing frantically, capturing the sounds that his ears are hearing.

ANOTHER ALONE: Exactly.

Me: So I'm in the listening hunt for a Mozart piece?

ANOTHER ALONE: Everybody is.

ME: Reminds me of something I once heard. Bach's music may be the music of heaven. But God listens to Mozart.

THE MUSIC OF THE SILENCE

All I'm hearing is silence. And my own noise. My own tuning, or screeching.

We need to become still if we are to hear the music. To take a few deep breaths. To feel the breath coming in and out of our bodies. We've got a technical problem here. How can you listen to the silence and to me at the same time? I think again of isolation. A feeling of sadness comes. You have to listen to the silence alone. Or to the silence coming through me. I am picturing you stopping from time to time as you read, pondering the thoughts and musings, bringing them into your own silence. Musings, music. Hmm.

Hum. Humming can open to music. I'm hearing in my silence a raucous old rock tune called "I Got the Music in Me." Music, and musings. From the muse. The muses were daughters of Zeus and Mnemosyne. Zeus, of course, was father of the gods. Mnemosyne, you might remember, is memory. The muses came to be through the joining of the father of the gods with memory. I don't know what to make of that. But I'm curious about the muses.

Hesiod said this about them: "They are all of one mind, their hearts are set upon song and their spirit is free from care. He is happy whom the Muses love. For though a man has sorrow and grief in his soul, yet when the servant of the Muses sings, at once he forgets his dark thoughts and remembers not his troubles. Such is the holy gift of the Muses to men [and women]."

I am remembering (Mnemosyne) David playing the lyre for King Saul who was terribly depressed. The music helped ease the sorrow and grief in his soul. Freed his spirit from care.

That helps me. We, too, are full of sorrow and grief. Another Alone, God, of whom Zeus was the Greek expression, invites us to open to the muses. To remember—I suddenly feel a movement, an agitation—that time, that place, that what? To remember the from which, the *ex nihilo*, where the music originates.

Originates is suggestive. Originate means to begin. Something can't begin in the deepest sense if it was before. It is just repeating, re-membering. Coming together again. What am I getting us into? Another Alone, God, is asking us to remember what hasn't been before. To call into the nothing for a muse to come. Remember. Member means a part—especially a limb—of the human body. From which we get dismemberment. And rememberment, yes?

It's getting a tad personal now. To remember could be to come together again in one's own body, one's own self. To remember could thus suggest becoming whole. Neurologist Oliver Sacks writes in his book *A Leg To Stand On* of an injury he sustained while mountain climbing. In simple terms, his leg just went dead, became other. He lost his connection to it. Where once was a leg, he now felt nothing. Creepy. Where once was a leg, now the nothing. He writes that "it was no longer a part of my 'inner image' of myself—having been erased from my body-image, and also my ego, by some pathology of the most serious and inexplicable kind."

Later, "The leg had vanished, taking its 'place' with it—I no longer remembered having a leg—I became all of a sudden desolate and deserted—" He had been psychically dismembered.

This has been happening forever. Another piece of music comes to mind. I hear tom-toms, drums beating in the forest. Think for a moment of Dante's dark wood before he enters hell. Drums beating. Tribal people with their healers, the shamans. Shamans, according to Eliade, are technicians of the sacred. How do they become such? By falling ill themselves. By going into a coma for an extended period, often for three to twelve days, during which time the sick person goes on an inner journey.

Typically, the person, usually a young teenager, has experiences of being dismembered by bad spirits. The spirits chop her (or him) up into little pieces. Some time later, good spirits put her back together, that is, re-member her. She may be taken to the tribal spirits, the Grandfathers, or Grandmothers, or some wise animal, and instructed that she has been chosen to be a healer.

When she awakens, the elder shaman is called. On hearing of her experience, the elder shaman takes her to study with him (or her) for five to ten years, so that she can learn the secrets of the herbs and the shamanic techniques. When she finishes her training, she becomes a healer, sent by the gods, or the Great Spirit, to her tribe. It is then her task to treat the sick with her newly learned skills, which include traveling into the inner world to rescue lost spirits.

Strange music. The healer who can heal is the one who was wounded, dismembered and re-membered. I return to Dr Sacks' book. The first words my eyes fall upon as I open the book are a quote from Novalis: "Every disease is a musical problem, every cure a musical solution." Now that's weird. I mean the finding of the quote right now, not the quote itself. Is the quote itself a gift from the nothing to help us along? Or did my fingers just present me with an interesting, quirky coincidence? Certainly, it was a coincidence, but has it any meaning?

And if it has meaning, what does that say about the world? Is there some force, some being, some something, that orchestrates (how about *that*?) events for the purpose of—what? Of helping the stranded soul? Advancing the soul further? Go another step with me. Is there, weirdness building on weirdness, an inner guide, a healer, a shaman who longs to return your lost soul? Can a soul be more lost than in hell?

But. But, but, but. A protest. If there are these meaningful coincidences, why don't they happen all the time? If they did, we'd call them cause and effect. You pray, you get well. Guaranteed. You didn't get well? Then you prayed wrong. Try again.

No. I can't buy it. For one thing, it's hardest to believe when you most need to. That's when you're most vulnerable to isolation. When you most need a shaman, someone who will travel into your hell with you, and rescue you. Or at least stay with you and try to help you figure out how to get on your way out of there.

I see Oliver Sacks as a shaman in this sense. He knows neurologic hell and thus can, at least to some degree, enter it with his patients. Because he has been through his own neurologic hell. Forced to struggle with questions like "Is this what I will have to put up with for the rest of my life? Will I never get the *feel* of true walking? Must everything be so complex—can't it be simple?"

Then healing came to him. Listen to the music. "And suddenly—into the silence, the silent twittering of motionless, frozen images—came music, glorious music, Mendelssohn, *fortissimo!* Joy, life, intoxicating movement! And, as suddenly, without thinking, without intending whatever, I found myself walking, easily—joyfully, *with* the music. And, as suddenly, in the moment that this inner music started, the Mendelssohn which had been summoned and hallucinated by my soul, and in the very moment that my "motor" music, my kinetic melody, my walking, came back—in this self-same moment *the leg came back*. Suddenly, with no warning, no transition whatever, the leg felt alive, and real, and mine, its moment of actualization precisely consonant with the spontaneous quickening, walking and music."

TRANSFORMATION EX NIHILO

True remembering. What did Sacks do to cause the healing? He sat in hell and struggled. Did he help his own healing along by his attitude? I don't know. He certainly didn't hurt it. For me, it is mystery. Grace. Music. A singing of the muses from the middle of the nothing, sent to ease his suffering, bereft, panicked soul. And to restore his body. A neurologic shaman is born, *ex nihilo*. What was, then was lost, now is again. What wasn't, now is. Transformation.

Norman Cousins enters my mind. In response to his supposedly incurable connective tissue disease, he took accepted medical treatment and added to it a treatment of laughter. He watched Marx Brothers movies, read joke books, and claimed that he laughed himself to full recovery. What is this? The music of laughter? Did laughter heal him? Has he discovered a new treatment for connective tissue disease?

Experts are sharply divided about this. Some say spontaneous remission is the best we can say. That we don't know why he got well. They certainly can't see laughter as a causative agent. Others think he opens a new door, that we need to explore the effects of laughter and other aspects of the mind carefully. In fact, they claim that they can already see and use some of these effects to bring healing.

I want to jump into the crevice between these two views. Maybe laughter created the conditions for healing to occur. Maybe it didn't *cause* the healing. Could it be that there is a mysterious music that sings in the nothing? That breaks through when it will, when it can, to bring wholeness?

But what about death? The ultimate defeat? The proof that all of this is, after all is said and done, nonsense? Because there is no healing of death?

Maybe there is. And here we get to the weirdest place of all. A place of laughter. At the fools who believe in the impossible. That is one kind of laugh. The other comes from the fools themselves. They have experienced something that releases them even from their fear of death. Something that comes from the middle of the nothing and defies even death. I am speaking of resurrection. Let's try now to open to that.

12

RESURRECTION

I drove with my family to Cape Cod yesterday. On the way, we were confronted with the results of Hurricane Bob. Trees lifted out of the ground, houses damaged, roadways littered with tree limbs though the main debris had been carried away. The power of nature. An act of God, as the insurance companies say. On the radio news we heard how expensive Bob was, costing almost a billion dollars.

A STORY OF RESURRECTION

A memory came to me. About resurrection. A re-membering. Two and a half years ago, a friend of mine lost his wife to cancer. Hers was a relatively quick death. Three months after diagnosis she was dead. They had had a vital relationship throughout their married life and he participated actively in her death.

Soon after her death, his mother-in-law died and he traveled to South Carolina for her funeral. While he was there, Hurricane Hugo smashed the coast. The morning after the hurricane, he came outside and surveyed the damage. Devastation was everywhere. Trees down, houses crushed. Great despair filled him. His beloved wife was dead. He was there to attend his mother-in-law's funeral. The world lay injured before him. "Is this the end?" he wondered aloud. "Is life over for me?" A terrible ache opened in him so that he felt he would die of the pain. Just then, a mother duck and her four ducklings came quacking out of a culvert, from under a fallen tree. Something stirred in him. Hope managed to show itself in the midst of the wreckage that so well symbolized his own soul.

Resurrection. New life coming out of the wreckage. Isn't it just a coincidence? Not according to him. Those silly ducks were messengers to him. Told him that everything was *not* over, that life had not been utterly defeated by destruction.

What about these two different responses to the arrival of the ducks? It is in musing, singing, about the ducks that our discussion of resurrection begins. The cynical person inside has to respond quickly to this claim of resurrection, that the ducks are only there coincidentally, at best a fortunate gift of chance.

Now here is something weird. I decided to look up "chance" in my etymological dictionary and found that chance is related to cadence, which is derived from the Italian *cadenza*, "itself taken over internationally, by music." Whoa! I don't claim to be a good etymologist, but chance is related to music? I couldn't resist turning next to "fortunate" as in the above "fortunate gift of chance." Fortunate comes from fortune, which has as its base the Latin *fors*, chance. A "fortunate gift of chance" becomes "chancy gift of music." Those ducks were a chancy gift of music.

Maybe resurrection is a chancy gift of music. That feels right to me. There is nothing we can do to cause resurrection. It is a chancy gift at best. But it adds melody to life. It gives a rhythm, a meaning, to life. At least it did to my friend as he stood in the debris of a hurricane, lifted from his misery by five stupid and wonderful ducks. Who maybe aren't stupid at that. They were, after all, smart enough to show up for the resurrection.

I may have offended a few Christians with this little image of resurrection. For Christians, resurrection is that momentous event when Jesus came back from the dead. Which for most people who aren't Christians is harder to swallow than the so-called meaningful arrival of the ducks. I personally believe that the two events are related. Not isolated. Which again reminds us that we are in hell.

Where, if I am correct, Another Alone moans. Just like my friend in South Carolina did. God moans, the ducks respond, resurrection. God moans, Jesus responds, resurrection. I don't think, for even a moment, that I have explained anything here. I'm just trying to set up a way to relate to you about resurrection. Because I suspect that it is crucial to the healing of hellish depression.

CHRISTIANITY

So this is now going to turn into a Christian thing? It looks like it, doesn't it? But remember Halloween and the cross. The "Christian thing" has been a part of this tale all along. I want to add, however, that my goal isn't to convert you to Christianity, but rather to converse with you. The "Christian thing" helps me to do this. You are, of course, perfectly free to reject what I say. But I hope you will answer me, rather than just leaving because resurrection sounds too ridiculous to you. That would push me further into isolation.

Besides, resurrection isn't only a Christian thing. It discloses a longing at the center of humanity. The pyramids are testimony to the Egyptian belief in life after death, for pharaoh. For eons many traditional cultures have used resurrection imagery at the beginning of the springtime. After the long and dark winter, the desperate call was made to the earth to awaken, to come alive again. To Persephone to return from Hades, to fructify the earth. How very frightening it would have been to them if the world hadn't awakened each springtime. Panic and then despair would have set in. For them, eternal winter would reign. C. S. Lewis depicts this in his children's book The Lion, the Witch, and the Wardrobe, where, due to a curse put upon the land by the white witch, it is always December but never Christmas.

There's the Christian thing again. My point is this. Resurrection pictures a longing older than Christianity that life go on beyond death. Whether that be the death of winter (we speak of "the dead of winter") or the death of a person. Life longs to be more than nothing. Each life strives to reproduce in some way, to stretch beyond its little self toward something more than itself. This is one reason for conversation. And for writing books, for that matter. We are desperately trying to reach out to others.

THE LONELINESS OF LIFE

Do you see what I'm getting at? There is a loneliness in life, an urge to unite with the other. A cry that it is hopeless, from the Voice of Aloneness. A moan from God that begs us not to give in to the Voice's words. A desire for life to wake up. "Wake up!" the pagans yelled at the sleeping earth. "Wake up! Be alive!" we want to yell at our lives, too. But we can't if we don't in some way believe in resurrection.

Of course, not everyone wants to be reborn. Many people so hate life that they are ready to leave it. They often help themselves along with pills, with weapons, in auto accidents. They are victims of the Voice of Aloneness.

I know this. It furthers my point. These poor people get lost in isolation. Lose their lives to despair. The Buddhists want to help these sufferers, by telling them that they can be freed from this world of suffering, this repeating cycle of death and rebirth. But not by suicide. By enlightenment. By showing the falseness of self that leads to suffering. By seeing beyond their suffering to the nothingness behind it. Only thus can the person be freed. By giving up everything. What a profound response to suffering! It comes from that same longing to move beyond hell, but goes in another direction than resurrection. It turns a different way. Helps people experience a different kind of conversion. One which can help them to grow.

REINCARNATION

I have been thinking a lot lately about resurrection and reincarnation. Wondering about its relationship to resurrection. Not seeking the Buddhist solution of enlightenment, but trying to enter the experiences of others.

Recall the dying man I worked with who believed in reincarnation. Had I been unable to enter his domain, I don't believe that I could have helped him to die creatively, rather than full of suicidal wishes. Or been helped with my own fear of death. Maybe I was converted, turned, in my conversations with him about death. Maybe my dying moment will be more peaceful because of entering the domain of reincarnation with him.

Many others who believe in reincarnation have come to talk with me. One woman made a tremendous breakthough during a workshop at which she came to the clear realization that she had lived before. She could even tell me about the specific horrors of those lives and how they infected her present life. As she dealt with her past lives, her present life began to improve markedly. *Quod agit existit*. Her belief acted. Something real was happening in her life.

Resurrection

She felt encouraged and hopeful. The aching depression of her life began to lift.

This presented me with an interesting problem. I didn't believe in reincarnation. But her experience showed me its power to change her life. I now know that there is *something* to reincarnation, something true. I've seen its transformative, freeing effects. I've seen the transformative effects of sharing one's metaphor and not being mocked. Like resurrection for me. If you mock my belief in resurrection, you isolate me. And truth be told, you seem like a hellhound to me, like a representative of the Voice of Aloneness, trying to push me under. More and more, it makes sense to me that conversion isn't a one-way street. I don't have *the* truth. Nor do you. Science has taught us that truth is gained gradually, through approximations.

THE DRAMA OF THE MOMENT

Whoa! That is only partly true. Remember Halloween, for me. Past lives, for my friend. It is important not to factor out the drama. The *resurrection*, I want to say. The momentous instant when reality changes. For good or ill. How about *that*? Is it unthinkable that resurrection could bring us to a negative place?

It is for me. A clarifying point. I don't believe that all transformation is resurrection. Even if all transformation (biased point this) suggests resurrection. Points to the longing for the beyond. The pothotic longing, the insatiable.

I have a thought. Maybe resurrection is the insatiable longing in us. Maybe built into our beings is the longing for being. For more than nothing. We are particles of life, striving to live. To *live*, not to die. Except that death is part of life. And so we long to die. But not into nothing. Why should I do anything, if it all ends in nothing? That doesn't seem intelligent to me. It seems a waste of time. But such certainties bring depression. Take away our energy. Settle into our bodies, which sometimes can only be shaken free by medications. Those real material pills that inform us, materialists that we are, that what is happening to us is real. Well, thank God and the pharmaceutical companies for the pills then. Because they not only cause a chemical conversion in our brains. They also tell us that what we are experiencing, hell, is in some sense real. And so we get better. At least, our bodies do. But our questions remain.

What is this all for? What does my life mean? What does *life* mean?

TWO ANSWERS TO OUR QUESTIONS OF MEANING

To me, belief in reincarnation suggests one answer. According to reincarnation, life is a process of enlightenment that happens over many lifetimes. Enlightenment, in the Buddhist sense, goes one step further. Through enlightenment one is freed from the wheel of life and death. One becomes free of life. One realizes that one's self is illusory. This stirs a sense of hopelessness in me as *The Bhagavad Gita* did years ago. Maybe this discloses my attachment to self. My unwillingness to sacrifice my individual being to the Absolute. I'm certain it does. I have no wish to deny the value of Buddhist enlightenment. I simply find myself, of necessity, in need of something other than the dissolution of self into the Absolute. I would make a lousy Buddhist.

Resurrection offers me something else. Resurrection is an explosion of God into being. And into individual being. It is a new moment. A totally new thing. Just like Buddha's enlightenment is a totally new "thing." Maybe the Buddha, the enlightened one, brought an Eastern resurrection, as it were, by freeing people from their separate selves. Whereas resurrection (to the extent that I can imagine it) frees the person, the self that dissolves in Buddhism, from the broken world by lifting the self to a new experience of life.

Christianity, as have pagan religions and Judaism through the ages, proposes that the material world is sacred, that our bodies are sacred and adds, through resurrection, that the goal of life doesn't exclude the body.

Resurrection acknowledges the value of the body, whatever else it does. It proclaims, to me at least, that bodies are part of the big picture. That rather than giving up self, we must uncover the true self. And this cannot be done until and unless we realize that bodies have eternal value.

Resurrection is a dramatic statement of the *something* of earthly life. Of the no of life to the nothing as absolute. It is an image and expression of what life is about. Thus, according to my understanding of resurrection, life is for becoming persons. Life is for embodiment. The body isn't bad. It is a crucial piece of the whole picture. Sexuality isn't bad, as the gnostics and many latter-day Christians believe. It brings life, it embodies new beings. And not only children. Because sex, intercourse, is a kind of conversation between people. Seeking to call both of them into deeper relational being. To call them out of isolation into the central purpose of life.

Try this. Resurrection, (I'm speaking of the particular resurrection of Jesus here and I'm not asking you to believe me), is the disclosure of life beyond isolation. Life, Jesus' resurrection says to me, is relational. How about saying it this way? Jesus came back to fill the world with his new discovery. From tales about him he seems to have been that kind of guy. And what was his new discovery? That there is life beyond murder and torture. That transformation comes even with death. Or can. That love wins.

The apostle Thomas, as told in John (20: 24–29), wasn't at Jesus' first resurrection appearance to the disciples. When they told him what had happened, he responded in effect: "You guys are turkeys of the first magnitude! There is no way you can get me to believe that nonsense. Unless I touch the wounds in his hands and feet, I won't believe." I'm glad that there was a skeptical representative at the beginning of things.

So what did Jesus do? He appeared again and invited Thomas to touch his hands and feet. He responded precisely to Thomas' doubt. He came to Thomas where he was and met him there. I'm reminded of hell and isolation again. And of that crazy cross after Halloween. In some profound way, that cross got to me like the wounds got to Thomas. I believed immediately, just as Thomas did. Though I didn't know what it was that I believed.

RELATIONAL RESURRECTION

What did I believe? That relation could break through my isolation. And more, that there was something going on in the nature of things that I had yet to imagine. Something wild and hopeful. And so I danced out of that office. Maybe my body was responding to the music that my mind could not yet imagine.

And this. Whatever the creed intended, the saying that "he descended into hell" touches me now. Suggests a truth that I don't fully understand. That I don't *begin* to understand. Here is the truth. There is relation even in hell. Or the *possibility* of relation in hell. It comes through moaning, and shrieking, and listening. It comes from being with each other. Something wonderful can break into hell, into depression and isolation. Resurrection isn't about immortality. It's about life. About the love at the core of life. About a reality that is alive, that acts, *agits*, agitates, creates, shakes us by our shoulders and calls us alive. There is something big going on here, something very hopeful for depressed folks. If it is true.

For resurrection proclaims that life somehow isn't defeated by death. That relationship isn't killed off by murder. That love isn't destroyed by hatred. Graham Greene's novel *Monsignor Quixote* ends with the title character celebrating the Mass while in a trance. He lifts the invisible host to heaven, then the invisible cup of wine. He offers communion to his beloved best friend, the Communist mayor of his town. Then Quixote falls over dead. The mayor wonders, "Why is it that the hate of man—even of a man like Franco— dies with his death, and yet love, the love which he had begun to feel for Father Quixote, seemed now to live and grow in spite of the final separation and the final silence—for how long, he wondered with a kind of fear, was it possible for that love of his to continue? And to what end?"

We don't know why this is so. But if it is so, don't we want to rejoice? For love can then come into our hell and isolation. If we can stand it.

13

DEPRESSION

It is four-thirty in the morning. I have been lying in bed thinking for almost an hour. The light of the full moon shining on the deck outside our room awakened me. As I lay quietly, thoughts about this chapter passed through my mind. Images of the inferno. All the possibilities that Dante thought of, and didn't. The relation of depression to hell. Curious wording, the relation of isolation.

THE LOST STARS

I brought several books with me to the Cape, including Dante's *Inferno* and a modern novel by Larry Niven and Jerry Pournelle of the same name. I have been rereading Niven and Pournelle's novel since I've been here. One of the things that strikes me about the novel is the variety of tortures imagined by Niven and Pournelle, most of which come from Dante.

This gets me to thinking about Dante's imagination. His poem is called the *Comedy*. If hell was the only territory through which he passed, it would have to be called Dante's *Disaster*. Again, a word play. *Aster* is Greek for star. Hell, as disaster, is separation from the stars. Depression is isolation from the stars. When we are depressed we are cut off from the universe, trapped in our own underground, unable to see the stars in the night sky. Another image: depression is like a night without stars, an unending night.

At the gateway into Dante's hell are the words: "Abandon hope all you who enter here." This is precisely the problem of depression. It makes us want to turn around and hustle out of hell. But that's not the way hell is set up. Once you're in, you're in. It's a one-way turnstile. The only way out is to go down, and down, to pass through.

As Dante passes through hell, led by Virgil, he discovers people caught in all manner of torture, supposedly befitting their earthly lives. One example. Just beyond hell's threshold are the souls who refused to make any choices in life. They are stung incessantly by hornets and wasps and rush around aimlessly, screaming frantically. When someone raises a flag, they rush to follow it, because they have no minds of their own. Virgil says to Dante, "This dreary huddle has no hope of death, / Yet its blind life trails on so low and crass / That every other fate it envieth." These are the people who have refused their unique fate, to paraphrase Helen Luke from her book *Dark Wood to White Rose*.

It is our fate to pass through hell. Do we stop among the hornets or pass on? We pass on, of course. What we soon discover is that there are hell-zones where people of like nature are assigned. Thus, the lustful are grouped together, the gluttonous, the angry, the violent, the fraudulent, the betrayers. And people are punished according to their particular sins on earth. Each has a peculiar punishment that goes on for all eternity.

This reminds me of depression. The sense of stuckness that comes with depression. The hellish sense of being caught by one image. Or, even pre-image, as in "I'll never get out of here. I am stuck forever here. There is no other place for me. No hope to find another place."

Depression is the place of no movement. In another sense, depression is a failure of imagination. A place where we are caught by the Voice of Aloneness, which drones quietly in the background, making sounds that have become so familiar that it seems to be our own hopeless mind speaking. But it isn't. It isn't our mind speaking, isn't our whole mind speaking. It is the Voice of Aloneness, which acts as if it were the only show in town.

MOVING THROUGH HELL

There is something perversely fascinating about passing through hell. We see this person dipped in pitch. That one running barefoot across a burning desert. And another scalded by burning blood. But to run through the desert forever? Or be dipped forever in pitch? Spare me. It is not only the heat of such images that is so dreadful. It is also the boredom. After a short time, the hot desert becomes hellish in another way. It just goes on and on and on. Until a person is crazy with hopelessness.

What kept Dante going is that he kept going. See? He continued to imagine. He didn't get caught in one image. Though he needed Virgil's help a few times not to. I think there is a key to escaping depression here. And that is to keep moving. Or to get moving. To do *something*. To move out of hopelessness and look at it from another angle. To see if it looks any different from a new vantage point. Remember again the woman I mentioned earlier who was depressed because of a failed love affair. She was stuck. And only got unstuck by a new, ridiculous image. A tow truck.

Ridiculous. This is an important word here. To the truly depressed person every suggestion seems ridiculous. Which is why some need to get goosed by medication. That's another ridiculous image, isn't it? To get goosed by medication. To have the medication sneak up behind you, grab your fanny, and make you jump. I'm being irreverent, aren't I? Sometimes you have to be. To shock another out of his foolish worship of his depression.

Worship? Does a depressed person *worship* depression? It doesn't feel like that. Rather, the depression overwhelms us, traps us. The depressed person knows that anyone caught in her particular depression would also be trapped.

That is a good and fair comment. But who cares about fair in the middle of hell? The point isn't to be a navel gazer about depression. Isn't to figure out why, in God's economy, in God's justice, we should have to suffer this way. The point is to look for a way out of the predicament. To get moving, and to keep moving.

The words at hell's entry come to me again. "Abandon hope all you who enter here." It's an appalling sign. Suggestive and powerful. But why must we believe it? I hate that sign. Something in me refuses to believe it. I won't abandon hope. I won't let myself get stuck. I won't become one dipped in pitch or forced to run barefoot through the burning desert forever. I want a changing picture, not a repeating one. I want something to start, not just to end.

We have to keep moving. We have to open to new images. We have to imagine our way through this. Not sit like a needle on a scratched record, playing the same two or three, two or three, two or three words over again, again, again. Depression is a failure of imagination. It is a capitulation to the Voice of Aloneness. To nothingness, which says that there is no more. That what you see is what you get. And you get this, burning pitch for all eternity. No. That is so cowardly.

What do I mean? Cowardly?

It strikes me that there is so much more to see in our inner hell, in our isolation, than one image. We don't go further because of a failure of heart, because of a lack of courage. The way out is the way through. It takes tremendous courage to walk on. And if our own hells are anything like Dante's, it's only going to get worse before it gets better.

I understand that this is a hard suggestion. A brutal one even. Unfair. But neither is it fair that you be stuck forever in the same rut, hearing the same bloody word from the Voice of Aloneness: "Hopeless, hopeless, hopeless."

That's self-fulfilling prophecy. Say "It's hopeless" ten times. Then ten thousand times. I guarantee that it *will* become hopeless. Say over and over again that there are no images that can free you and you'll be right.

But no! I won't buy it. I can't accept that even the lost are ultimately lost. Though I, too, become a broken record if I stand in front of someone who says, "It's hopeless, it's hopeless, it's hopeless" and answer, "No it's not, it's not, it's not."

You know what happens then? Probably *I'll* get depressed. This is one of the reasons we need to keep moving. Why I need to say to you, "Come on and walk with me. Get up out of the burning pitch. Tell me about it as we walk."

IMAGES OF HELL

Am I contradicting something I said earlier? Didn't I say something about sitting with the person in hell? Both of these images strike me as true. A word about images. A sleight of hand, you might say. Each image has its own way, its own pattern, its own power. If a particular image depresses you, you've got to do something with it. You have to open it. This may mean moving deeper into it. You really can't get out of hell by going back. Or, it may mean leaving that image as unhelpful, getting towed out of it, so that you can go deeper into hell and find your way out. This is why (one of the reasons anyway) we need others to help us, Virgils to guide us along our way. Otherwise, we are so easily hypnotized by the Voice of Aloneness, droning the same hellish message over and over again. "Hopeless, hopeless, hopeless."

So where *is* the hope in this? T. S. Eliot in *"Four Quartets"* warns us "to wait without hope for hope would be hope for the wrong thing." To me, the hope is in going even deeper into hell, in learning the particular configurations of your own personal hell.

The hope is in seeing the configurations and particularities with another, rather than being eaten up by them alone. No wonder you don't want to go any deeper, if boiling blood is already being poured over your head. It's hard to imagine anything positive, as that blood scalds you. Once more, a major part of hell, of depression, is the stuckness and hopelessness. The very nature of where you are prevents hopeful images from having any reality for you.

This is very hard business, traveling through hell, breaking out of old images, old hopelessness, old patterns that lead us into despair again and again. For some of us, hell is a large place. We have so isolated ourselves that it takes a lifetime (or many lifetimes, if you believe the reincarnationists) to get through hell. If we get through at all.

But if we don't, then it *is* hell. As in eternity. As in stuck in the same place. As in a failure to imagine.

Am I annoying you? Getting on your nerves? Buzzing around you like a mosquito? Or am I stirring just a little bit of hope? Am I offering something at least partially believable by acknowledging that you are in hell, stuck in one place, in need of a tow or a jumpstart? Or of being left alone. Or of telling me your story. What it's like to be hung by your fingers for all eternity over a vat of boiling water. Because nobody listens. Everybody is too caught up in their own pain. Too busy burning, screaming, aching, and ailing to pay any attention.

Here is isolation again. The drama of the isolated one never gets told. Because nobody is there to listen. Listening opens up a world. Opens the doorway to your pain. Makes possible your descent into the depth of yourself. Or, contra Dante, shows you a hidden doorway out of hell. I'm not against such hidden doors. They are images, too. Your way and Dante's may be different.

HELL AS A PART OF LIFE

Or you may have to come to hell again and again. Or your hell may have oases in it. Resting places for the weary traveler. One thing seems certain to me. (Beware of certainty!) And it is this. Once entered, there is an eternal aspect of hell. The person who has entered hell can't forget it, has it as one of her reference points. Is vulnerable to it, particularly in emotionally trying times. Old hopelessness can jump on her when she's most vulnerable, and pull her back into the fiery swamp.

What do we do with this? Rant and rave about the unfairness of life? That's okay, and sometimes helpful. Do we give up? That plops us right back into hell, into stuckness. Hopefully, (note the word) we begin to learn how to negotiate hell. Maybe somebody gives us a crazy cross, or lets us know that we aren't totally unheard or isolated, as it has seemed. Maybe someone incarnates Another Alone, and lets out a groan for us. There are many possibilities. Note this word, too. Like hopefully, it doesn't capitulate to hell. Possibilities defy stuckness.

My experience is that hell is a part of life. Yours may be different. Don't get caught in my imagery. Cast it aside if it doesn't help you. It may be—I can imagine this—that you don't have to spend time in hell. If that's the case, hooray! *If* those around you aren't put into hell thereby. It could be that you are making life hellish for others, isolating them because you are unwilling to relate to the painful things of their lives. Because it might push you into hell. Hard business life.

Let me try again. My experience is that hell is a part of life. That it has much to teach us. Which isn't to say we should blithely search out hell so that we may learn from it. Hell is there already. In your isolated places, in your forgotten places. Victims of the Holocaust insist that we never forget the horrors they went through. Because if we do, we are doomed to repeat them. More importantly, if we forget, we negate their experience, we isolate them still again, we put them into psychic killing camps.

One more time. My experience is that hell is a part of life. That we must travel through it if we are ever to escape it. I want to share something with you which might help me make the point I'm having trouble getting to.

MEETING AN OLD MONSTER AGAIN

Several years after my Halloween experience, I published a book entitled *Masters of The Heart*. In it I wrote of my journey away from agnosticism to find a spiritual perspective. Near the end of the book, after exploring several philosophies and modern science, I imagined entering a cave that turned out to be the very labyrinth where the mythical Minotaur waited for people who got lost underground and then devoured them. The Minotaur of mythology, you may know, was a beast, half-human, half-bull.

In my imagery, I was lost in the labyrinth and suddenly confronted by the Minotaur. My monster had certain peculiarities that differentiated it from the mythological monster, most notably, four heads positioned so that he could look in all directions at once. I felt overwhelmed by the beast and imagined a young man entering the cave to rescue me. The imagery worked. I was freed from my fear with his arrival and his stern words to the monster. Then he led me out of the cave. I needed to call this other figure because I had stumbled upon something inside me that I couldn't handle alone. I didn't feel strong enough in my isolated self to face the monster. If I had been strong enough to do so, experience has shown me that the other would have instructed me to do so.

Fifteen years later, a few months ago, I came in touch with that monster again. This time my task was different. I was ready to face the monster. In the *Inferno*, the first being that Dante and Virgil encounter when they enter the circles of the violent is the Minotaur. As I came to face my own inner violence again, the same proved true for me. My four-headed monster appeared. I was now ready to face this part of me. The one in me who looks critically in all directions, who devours all my creative thoughts, who keeps me lost in my labyrinthine imagination. The one who devours the new life that others share with me, who is critical and hostile. I could now face him, now accept that he lives in me and acts. *Quod agit existit.*

I rediscovered the monster at my twenty-year college reunion. It happened on Sunday morning at the end of the weekend, as I sat looking out the window at Notre Dame's beautiful campus. My wife lay sleeping in bed. We had seen old friends for two days and shared memories and new stories with them. Now, as I stared at the campus, a powerful feeling came over me. I wanted to bellow out my window. I wanted to rip off the polite face of the reunion and scream at the trees and buildings. The monster wanted me to cry out, to be seen. I didn't scream out the window.

But I did scream into my journal. As I look at my journal and reread my words, I am reminded how unhappy I was during college. As I've already said, I didn't know who I was in college or where I was going. Then Halloween came.

Twenty years after Halloween, the unexpressed monster appeared as he had fifteen years earlier. He was bellowing inside me. When I finally faced the monster and asked him what he wanted, he said these words to me: "I am a monster lost in a cave."

Another Alone then told the monster that I was sent to get him, to *see* him, to get to know him. This did not make me happy at all. Nor did the command: "You must love the monster."

This is exactly what I didn't want to do. I wanted to lose the monster, to bury him again. But hadn't I done that for twenty years already? And here he was again, a four-headed, yelling horror show. I decided it was time to face him. When I did, to my surprise, I felt tremendous compassion for him. I sensed the loneliness he had endured these many years. I realized that he *was* lost in the labyrinth, that he was so hungry for people that he devoured them when they came his way.

My task was now clear. I realized that he had not devoured me fifteen years earlier, that I had been protected from him. Now I was ready to lead him from the labyrinth. I took his hand and brought him out of the underground cave. Just as the young man had brought me out so many years before.

Suddenly, he and I emerged from the cave and were standing in a field looking up at the night sky. At millions of stars. I heard him moaning with delight at the glorious night. As I listened to his sounds, it was as if I were seeing the stars in a new way. As if they were crying out both to me and to the monster to be. They repeated their cries again and again until I felt us both reconnecting to the stars.

I was experiencing a *re*aster. The end of a dis-aster. Because I had opened myself to my monster. That fact shocked me awake. My monster, my violent one, long hidden underground, reconnected me to the stars when I invited him to leave his hidden place and come into my world.

What does this suggest to us? That we should be clobbering each other with our monsters? That we should be devouring one another in our hunger? No. In fact, we must do just the opposite. We must *see* the monster in us who destroys others and take him (or her) into our arms. We must claim our monsters as our very own, as blood of our blood, as part of our very beings. When we do this, the disaster ends. We emerge from our underground hiding places. And there waiting for us, as they always have been, are the stars.

Can you imagine entering your hidden monstrous places? To do this is to move through hell rather than staying stuck in your repeating images of depression. Does it give you courage to know that waiting for you when you finally emerge are the shining stars? Lights shining in the middle of the darkness?

14

EUCHARIST

I had intended to entitle this chapter "Christ." I had intended to explore the relationship of Christ to hell. But I had several false starts. Sadly, the term is accurate. There has been something false about these attempts to write about Christ. Something false that pointed out the truth to me. The truth relates to my cowardice, to my desire to please, to my fear of rejection. So I find myself suddenly with a great opportunity. I can go to a place of deep isolation and share it with you.

Last night's dream interrupts. There was a meeting in a large stadium to honor a young man who joyfully gave his goods to the poor. No fuss, no egocentricity. I watched him without envy, though I couldn't understand how he could be so magnanimous. I've worked with dreams for over fifteen years. I could now hide behind the dream if I chose to. I could talk about the emergence of a generous young man in myself. But that would be to succumb to temptation, to avoid a greater good by talking about a lesser good.

I intend now to write a dialogue with Jesus. I intend to set it in hell. I intend to call him into the midst of my falseness. I want to share with you how the imaginative process works, as it works. And I don't want to. I'd rather do it didactically, by using examples. I don't want to be the frog pinned on the dissecting table. I want to be the teacher. But that seems false. The image amuses me. People are trudging along through hell. As they come around a curve, a man stops them and says, "I am going to teach you about hell. I will tell you how to make your way through it and how to avoid the dangers so you can escape."

Some wiseguy from the crowd shouts, "If you're so smart, why are you still in hell? Why don't you lead us out?"

The teacher is another temptation. And false. I could do it that way. But in hell the teacher is the doer, the agitator, the struggler.

I want very much to talk to you about Jesus. And, I want very much to *avoid* talking about him. Many of the people who talk publicly about Jesus are obnoxious twits. Sorry, but that's the way I feel. I find them sanctimonious, proud, too sweet for my taste, and condescending as hell.

I'm now musing that maybe I'm one of the poor people that young guy in my dream can help. Musing. Maybe I can use my dream as the form. Identify that young man with Jesus. He could be. He has the right credentials. He's giving, not egotistical, teaching me in a straightforward way. And I don't recognize him. But to do that feels like another temptation. It's not naked enough.

As I was making my coffee this morning, I wondered how to proceed with this chapter. There were several interior car wrecks as thoughts rushed in from all sides. When I thought of just dialoguing, something settled in me. But not my heart. It started to beat faster.

"That's what I have to do," I thought. "I have to share a dialogue. Get Jesus to talk. Let Jesus speak directly in me." The disbeliever in me was angry at this, fuming. The shy one started searching desperately for an out. How could he avoid the exposure? Several voices begin speaking now.

A DIALOGUE WITH MYSELF

A Helpful One speaks: You could do the dialogue privately, in a hidden corner of hell, then present your results to them. Share only what you want to. Or nothing at all, if it proves too embarrassing.

My Ego Self: But if I do that, I might as well forget it. I'll be hiding my most hidden self. I'll be lying to people. Telling them they have to open up. But I'm not opening up myself.

A Defensive One: They'll mock you. They'll laugh at you.

My Ego Self: Maybe. That's why all the false starts, why I'm having such a hard time. I've got to do it this way.

A Defensive One: Damn.

My Ego Self: But how about this? I'll be wide open since that's the only way to do these things with any benefit. Afterwards, if it truly harms you, I won't share it. And we'll have a new encounter with Jesus.

A Defensive One: Don't say that name so loud. They'll think you're one of those converters.

My Ego Self: You don't like them, do you?

The dialogue is quickly settling out. The two figures are a defensive part of me that I now name the Shy Angry One (SAO) and my ego self whom I'll call the Listener (L).

SAO: I hate them. They give me the creeps. I remember being at the beach in California twenty years ago. That young creep, who was about fifteen, came up to me and asked me if I'd found Jesus. I wasn't clever enough to say, "I didn't know he was lost." I wasn't brave enough to say, "Get the hell out of here. I'm trying to relax on the beach." So I asked him a question. "What about evil? If the world is saved, what about all the terrible things that still happen?" You remember what he did?

L: Yeah.

SAO: He said, "Wait a minute. I've got to ask my leader." Then he trotted off to some twenty-year-old, or forty- year-old, with my question. It felt good for a minute. "The idiot," I thought. "He doesn't know what he's doing. When he comes back, I'll throw Halloween in his face."

L: You decided not to.

SAO: I was afraid they'd perform an exorcism right there on the beach. He came back finally. Started to spew some answer. I can't remember what he said, but it really angered me. I wanted to yell at him. "Get the hell out of here!" Or get into an argument with him. Shake his shoulders and cry out to him, "Do you really believe this stuff? If you do, take me on. Don't press your sweet smile in my face. Encounter me as a human being. Tell me about you. Tell me what got you into this stuff. Convince me. Be passionate. Tell me about being a junkie, getting some girl, or ten girls, pregnant to prove what a stud you are. Tell me how your parents beat you. Anything but this sweetness. It's enough to make me gag."

L: Angry.

SAO: Yes.

L: Your anger's good.

SAO: I doubt that. Don't you start getting on my case, too. Don't you try to convert me to health.

L: I'm not trying to. I'm listening. I'm touched by your story. You're telling me why you're in hell.

SAO: So?

L: Say it.

SAO: When are you going to laugh at me? Mock my struggle. Say, "There, there, child, it's a mystery. You can't understand it. And God loves you. If you're a good boy, you'll be with God forever in heaven." Well, as you can see, I'm not in heaven. I'm in hell, covered with burns and blisters.

L: I know.

SAO: One of the damned.

L: Me, too.

SAO: Really?

L: Look at the burns all over my face.

SAO: Yeah. You do have lots of burns. So why aren't you yelling? Are you one of those tricky demons who gets people's hopes up, then shoves them back into the fire?

L: Nope. Just another one of the damned. You're helping me.

SAO: Come on. How can I be helping you?

L: You're talking to me. You're being honest. You're reminding me where I am. You're touching my own isolation. I'm a lot like you.

(The Shy Angry One's face opens a tentative smile.)

SAO: How's that?

L: I'm lost, too. Isolated. I listen to other people's soul pain. Have a hard time sharing my own.

SAO: You don't have all the answers?

L: Hah! I'm sorry. You jumped about a foot.

SAO: I thought you were going to hit me.

L: No. I wanted to tell you I understand your suffering because I'm a lot like you are. I hide my shy person, you, so that people won't see how lost I am.

SAO: It helps me to be with another lost person here. Somebody who admits he's lost. That's a good start.

L: Tell me.

SAO: Because it's the truth. I . . .

L: Go on.

SAO: You were talking.

L: Talk for me.

SAO: I was angry at that California kid because he was so certain about what to do with questions. He wasn't there. He was a saved robot. It infuriated me.

L: Why?

SAO: Because he excluded me. He excluded my struggles. Gave an answer too quickly and didn't wait to hear about where I was. Reminds me . . .

L: Of?

SAO: Earlier teaching.

L: Tell me.

SAO: They shut off all my good questions by saying they were mysteries.

L: What questions, child?

SAO: Why do you call me child? I'm twenty-two years old.

L: I wanted to say "son." Felt shy about it.

SAO: Call me son. I like it better.

L: Go ahead, son.

SAO: My favorite question, the one that bothered me most had to do with eternity. Eternity made my stomach queasy. You can't use eternity up. And worse . . .

L: Go ahead.

SAO: Our catechism taught us that God always was, is, and will be.

L: Yeah.

SAO: If God always was, how could the present get here? You could never use up all that eternity before now. Each before would still have an eternity before it all the way back to forever which still has a forever before it.

L: It still intrigues you.

SAO: It still upsets my stomach.

L: Mine too. So you thought about eternity. What happened?

SAO: When I asked about it, you know what answer I got?

L: Yep. It's a mystery.

SAO: Exactly.

L: It's a wonderful mystery, son. One to open up. It makes me think about eternity, about the imponderables. About the two kinds of time. Chronos and kairos. Why are you crying?

SAO: Because you're taking me seriously. Not shutting me up with mystery words. You're opening to the mystery with me.

L: Because you help me.

SAO: You want to know something else that bothered me a lot?

L: Sure. What?

SAO: First communion.

L: Tell me.

SAO: I remember the monsignor telling us that his first communion day was one of the two happiest days of his life. The other was his ordination.

L: Go on.

SAO: I went to the altar with great excitement. Something big was going to happen.

(The shy one's face clouds over.)

L: What's the matter?

SAO: I just thought of something. The big thing that happened to me was Halloween. Not communion.

L: That's hard. Tell me about your first communion and I'll tell you about mine.

SAO: Did anything happen at yours?

L: I'll tell you. But go ahead with your story first.

SAO: Nothing *happened. The wafer stuck to the roof of my mouth. Nothing happened. No Jesus. If it was a mystery, it was an empty one. I didn't tell anyone because I figured I'd done something wrong. Or Christ had decided not to come to me. Whatever the reason, it was a big disappointment. The very biggest deal came up empty for me. Another memory.*

L: Tell me.

SAO: The next year a new kid came to school in the middle of the year. He wasn't Catholic, as we later found out. Every morning we started the school day with Mass. When one of the holy guys, you know the ones who went to communion on days that weren't Fridays, got up and went to communion, Jerry, the new kid, asked him when he returned to the pew, "What did they give you?" This brought some real excitement to us, let me tell you. We set out on a conversion crusade. We told him it was the body of Christ, the bread of heaven. Well, he started to go to communion every day. Until one of the sisters found out that he wasn't Catholic. We never saw him again at school.

L: He was expelled?

SAO: That's what I figure. I don't know. I don't know if I made up some explanation or if our teacher actually told us what a horrible thing Jerry had done. A non-Catholic person taking communion. Horrors! But you want to know something?

L: Yeah.

SAO: I think that's who communion should be for.

L: Me too.

SAO: You do?

L: Listen to my story of first communion. I was about your age, maybe twenty-four or -five. I was at Mass. At communion time, the priest turned around and said to the congregation as he held up the host, "Those of you who feel unworthy to come to communion, know that communion is for you especially. Come." I went. As I walked up, tears filled my eyes. I felt invited to communion for the first time. I felt that the priest was speaking directly into my soul. I hoped there were others walking up with me who felt the same way. Who were coming to communion for the first time. I wanted to know who they were. To grab them up in my arms and swing them around. To yell, yippie! To sit with them and hear their stories. To tell them mine. Just like we're doing now. Because what we're doing now, son, is what I have always longed for.

(The two men stand. Neither moves for a moment. The shy one opens his arms, welcomes the listener to come to him. The listener rushes to him and embraces him. Finally, he has found a teacher here in hell. One who teaches life. It is another first communion. In a dark corner, another sits quietly. The listener can barely discern the figure nodding.)

This is not at all what I expected when I started this chapter. Imagination is like that. If you give yourself to it, it often surprises you. I learned early in my life that imagination can't be controlled by me. Here is a typical example from my childhood.

I fantasized sports situations, which provided me with opportunities to be the hero. In my fantasy, I am standing at the foul line. It is the end of the basketball game. Just two seconds left. My team is losing by one point. If I sink both free throws (you see, I'm back in it), we win the game. The first shot is up. No! It hits the front of the rim and falls away. If I make the second shot, we'll go to overtime. I'll be the hero then. The second shot is up. It bounces off the back rim. The other team gets the rebound. We lose. Wait! The guy was standing on the out of bounds line. There's one second left. Time for a quick jump shot. The ball is passed to me. My shot is up. It's no good! I just couldn't force that stupid ball into the basket. Not in the critical fantasy situations. The important thing to me now, and then too, is that I recognized that there was another world there. But I didn't know how to share it with anyone. I couldn't say to my friends, "Do you ever have troubles in your hero fantasies, making the ball go into the basket? You don't? I give up. What kind of stupid question is that? You tell me."

Though it wasn't my goal (I see the pun) to write this dialogue, it opens our discussion for us. It frees me to talk more honestly about Christ (I hope).

How about you? What inner dialogues are going on in you right now? Do you recognize a shy one, a disbeliever? An angry one? A lonely one who has never spoken to anyone, even to you? If you do, will you turn to that one now? Will you open up a dialogue? Listen to what is stirring in you. It is time for that disbeliever, that shy one, that angry one, that unheard one to speak. Find the one most trapped in hell inside you. The one who wants most (and least) to speak. Ask her what she needs before we go ahead. Ask him how he feels about this Christ business. Maybe you're Jewish, or Buddhist, or atheist. Maybe Christ imagery offends you. That is all right. I'm not trying to convert you. I want to enter into conversation with you. To be turned by you. To turn you. We can't do that if we don't come. And everyone is invited. Especially the one who feels unworthy, or shy, or lost. Even the one with all the answers is invited. All of them. Bring them. Come.

15

CHRIST

I have been working on this chapter for two hours. I just erased six pages. Gone. Now I'm starting over. For several days now, I've been trying to get here. To talk about Christ. Because the cross is central to my story. And Jesus is.

I am in a quandry. I am full of feelings. Defensiveness. The cynicism of the Voice of Aloneness. The shyness of the young man in the last chapter. Concern for others who are caught in hell. Wanting to say to them, to you, try this. But not wanting to shove it in your face. That would be another hellish experience for you. I want to find the courage to say what is in me. And the insight to see what is inside me to say. Now, when I most want to fly, I feel grounded. By my cowardice, uncertainty, and anger.

What do I know? I know that Halloween happened to me. That friends helped me, but couldn't free me. That understanding and a cross enabled me to take a step in hell, but didn't catapult me into heaven. Opened me to the fact of hell. And to the desire of the universe not to leave me there.

What do I know? That Jesus was a lover, an imaginer, a practical visionary who saw the possibility of God manifesting in everyday life. That he was a radical who took on the religious establishment. And lost.

I want to sit there for awhile. Not rush to resurrection. To sit in the defeat. Imagine having a vision that God wants to come into the middle of human life in a totally new way. Imagine that you feel called to announce this great news and to help bring it into being. And that you fail miserably.

I don't want to run ahead to Christianity either. I'm thinking of the person Jesus. To have something so magnificent to share, yet not be able to convince others. To believe it so much that even in failure he stays with it. Remains true to it. Even as they clobber him.

Flannery O'Connor, the great Southern author, wrote that the South is Christ haunted. The phrase strikes a cord in me. I am Christ haunted. I thought of O'Connor at that moment because an image came into my mind. One that haunts me. That I hate. That makes me sick. It is the image of one person pounding a nail into another person's wrist. The image makes me think that we truly are in hell. Already.

How does a person do that to another person? Take a wrist and hold it against a board and bash a nail through it? In one of her books Annie Dillard wonders why people don't wear crash helmets to church instead of hats because of the power they are confronting. I wonder why people don't throw up in church during Holy Week when the crucifixion story is read. Why people don't run out of church screaming at the horror of it.

Hellish, that cross. Is that why it touched me so deeply? Here's a guy worse off than I am. Someone has driven nails into him. Why didn't I run out that professor's office in horror when he offered me a cross? Why instead the sudden surge of life?

THE SURGE OF LIFE

I don't know why it touched me so. I'm glad it did. There is some great mystery there.

At this moment, I feel another surge of new life. I want to try to share it with you. But I can't hold onto it. When I'm in my office with someone who loses an important thought, I say "Interrupt whatever we're saying and throw it in the second you remember it." That's what I'll do here, if words for the mystery return.

Curious to feel this surge of new life. While talking about something that makes me sick. Crucifixion isn't a pristine event. There is blood and sweat and torn skin here. A guy who has totally failed. And silence. Feeling a surge of new life in response to crucifixion is a mystery so great that it needs to be savored.

Terrible word, savored. Why does the word come to me now? How can we savor such a mystery? Do savor and save come from the same place? When I look up savor, I am referred to sage, which tells me nothing helpful. Doesn't suggest a connection between

savor and saved. Maybe the sage, the wise one, grows in wisdom by
savoring the mystery.

But such an awful mystery. We've made of it salvation, or discovered salvation there. Where has that surge of life I felt a few minutes
ago gone? I feel my isolation again. Hell. Something like the cross is
necessary to get our attention in hell. To enter hell with us.

Jesus knew hell. If hell is isolation and rejection. When he yelled
the line from Psalm 22 while he was hanging on the cross, "My God,
my God, why have you forsaken me" he expressed it.

I'm blocking again. Trying to. The words "lost brother" come to
me. A lost brother hanging there on the cross. Nothing I can do for
him. Except welcome him to hell. That certainly isn't the mystery
that brought me the surge of life. Hell doesn't seem mysterious at all
right now. Hell is just the way life is.

CONNECTION

What if I turn my imagination to him and speak with him? What if I
say, "Jesus, what is the surge here? Why am I suddenly filled with
life as I look at this disgusting image now? Or twenty years ago,
when I was given the crazy cross?"

What if I wait silently for an answer? Don't move or write until an
answer comes?

I don't hear anything. I feel agitated. Something is acting. An
image presents itself. I'm looking at his wrist. Remembering that the
nailed hand can't support the weight of a body. So the nail was
driven into the wrist instead of the hand. A pragmatic decision
based on Roman experience with killing.

I recognize one in me that would like to kill him off. Get rid of
him. And the cross. It's just too disgusting. But I'm Christ haunted.

More silence. I ask him again. "What is the surge of life I felt a few
minutes ago?" I hear an answer this time. He is speaking in my
imagination.

Jesus: Connection.
Me: Huh?
Jesus: Connection.
Me: I heard you. I don't understand.
Jesus: Connection. Don't look it up. Feel it. That's your answer.
Connection. The surge of life comes from the feeling of connection.

Yes. I still don't understand, but yes. On Halloween I discovered my disconnection, was dismembered. With that crazy cross I felt connection, was re-membered. Brought back from isolation. Had my isolation opened up. Discovered at the middle of me that I'm not alone. Even if I didn't understand. It made me feel like dancing. Like I heard a bit of the music.

Dancing isn't understanding, is it? It's not standing at all. It's moving. As in being alive. Dancing is a way of getting unstuck.

People have been dancing since there were people. People dance at celebrations. Music is played at celebrations. Weddings, bar mitzvahs, graduations. Music, yes. It takes away the isolation. It fills the air, stirs it. Moves people to move. That's my response to connection. To dance, to move.

There is no dancing on a cross, though. Death comes by suffocation. The weight of the body pulls it down so the crucified one can't breathe. He forces himself to stand up on the cross to take a breath. Has to pull against the nails. More tearing.

Are you dancing? Feeling any connection? Does this reach into your isolation in any way?

I worry at how poorly I'm expressing myself. That I might be serving isolation with my words rather than connection.

The question comes to me. Who was this guy that got crucified? I feel a nervous surge of energy in response. He was a guy who told stories about life. About God's eagerness to enter life. About God's presence in life, waiting to be discovered. He was a guy who liked peasants. Who ate with sinners. Who associated with outcasts. Who rejected anything that caused isolation.

That's good. Maybe he'd come to a dinner party in hell. Spend some time with us isolated ones. Break bread with us. Drink a little wine. Not treat us like outcasts. Wouldn't that be something?

Connection. I can't make you feel it. I can only suggest it and hope that the mystery happens for you. For us. Between you and me. So that we can begin relating in a new way. See that the outcast in each of us is not cast out. Is not a demon, but a waif, an orphan, who needs to be welcomed.

Do you know the famous story about a kid who came up and tried to talk with Jesus and the apostles chased the kid away? Jesus was indignant. Stopped what he was doing. Took the kid into his lap and turned the tables on the grownups. "Unless you become like this kid, you can't get into heaven," he said to them. Maybe the same thing is true of the waif. Unless you find your lost one, your beggar, the outcast in you, whom you try mightily to hide from yourself and others, you aren't going to escape hell. You're going to become more and more isolated.

Could that be the surge of life? The recognition that God wants me to be *me*? That I'm already accepted? That hell isn't forever, no matter what the experts say? Because God loves us. Comes to where we are. Is already where we are. As soon as we acknowledge this, hell opens up. We begin to discover that our isolated place is teeming with figures who want to be known. And there, too, is one like Christ, a human being, an other, who wants to connect us to ourselves. To others. To God.

16

COWARDICE

As I mentioned in the last chapter, I have been struggling with my writing about Christ. Unable to get it right, unable to get comfortable enough with my own position to say it clearly. Comfortable is an interesting word. From com-fort, meaning with strength. We are comfortable when we are in a position of strength.

I don't feel like a strong Christian. Or a certain one. This is curious since I have found new life through the central image of Christianity, the cross. It's as if I was given new life and left with my old struggles. With my old me. With the agnostic who doesn't believe half the stuff the Church says. At the same time, there is the believer who says there *has* to be something. This has to be for something, or else life is idiocy. Is "sound and fury . . . signifying nothing." I can't stand that. And it may be so.

CERTAINTY

I live with uncertainty. One reason I find many fundamentalist people annoying is that they seem so blasted certain. And then they push their certainty at me. Telling me that they know the way. That if I would be saved, I must go their way. Follow their interpretation as truth. And they can be so bloody insistent.

I think of William James' comment in *Varieties of Religious Experience* to the effect that proselytizers expose their own struggles with disbelief by the energy they expend trying to convert others to their position. It feels like that to me, too. I can't give myself to make them comfortable.

But I don't know. They may be right. Maybe the whole thing is certain. This is the power of my own uncertainty.

My mind shifts to people whose certainty doesn't bother me, but rather invites me. I'm thinking of those who have had near-death experiences. You know the ones I mean. You've read of the people who, after being in an accident or having a heart attack, are clincially dead for a few minutes. As medical personnel work desperately to bring them back, they enter another dimension, another reality.

Those who have had experiences while their hearts were stopped tend to report similar kinds of events. A typical experience might begin with the person floating out of his body and rising to the ceiling where he looks down on the people who are trying to resuscitate him. He then feels himself being pulled through a tunnel. Then loved ones who have died come to greet him. A being of light may appear whose great love transforms him, giving him a sense of peace he has never before known. There may be an instantaneous life review with this being, in which the person is suffused with a feeling of profound forgiveness. At some point, the person is told that he has to return to his body. Perhaps his child or wife still needs him. Perhaps there is work still to do. On return, such people typically state that they have lost their fear of death. They *know* there is an eternity. They have certainty. There is a peace that passes our understanding.

Why do I respond so positively to these people when other certainties anger me so? Why does one certainty feed me while another isolates me? A big difference between the two groups I'm considering is this. One group comes up to me on the beach and asks me if I've been saved. Implies that I could be lost if I don't follow their way. The other group tends to be silent about their experience because so few people ever believe them. They just live the rest of their lives without fear of death. They have no need to convert others to their position. Their belief isn't dependent on the affirmation of another person.

I want that. I fear I am more like those people who try to convert others because the belief or disbelief of another has a profound effect on me. To be in the presence of one whose knowing invites rather than demands soothes me, opens me, dares me to believe. Because this one enters my isolation with peace, not a club. Desperate certainty isn't certainty at all. It is a cry of isolation. Seen thus, my heart can go out to fellow isolates. Without my having to believe their expressions of isolation as my truth.

I remember working with a woman who had lived a life of profound spiritual isolation. Events from her life shamed her. She was certain that God had rejected her and she lived in dread of death. Fearing the moment when she would come before God who would damn her for all her earlier transgressions.

She tried desperately to be good, and in fact, in act, succeeded. But her heart didn't change. She didn't want that goodness. She wanted to live, to be vital and passionate, but she didn't dare. As she became comfortable being herself with me, she began to face this deep desperation. She searched and struggled and shook with fear for years.

One night she had a dream that a holy man was caressing her breasts, accepting her, calling her to be. From that moment, something changed. A conversion happened. She turned. She began to know that God called her to be herself. That life wanted her to be her truest being.

A different kind of certainty came. A certainty of an alive person pushing on, daring, climbing the next mountain, facing the next fear. Gradually, in an unfolding way, she discovered what people who have near-death experiences realize in an instant. The core of life is trustworthy.

Another piece of her story speaks to the journey through hell which we are here imagining. Each new turn in the road brings with it her old fear. But the fear doesn't hold. As she struggles with her fear, life opens. It again proves to be trustworthy and she walks on.

FEAR

I want to change the title of the chapter from "Cowardice" to "Fear," at least for a moment. The word coward derives from the Latin *cauda, coda,* meaning a tail. Cowards are people whose tails are tucked between their legs. Fear derives from the Old English *faeran,* meaning to terrify. This points to fear in its noun form, meaning fright, dread. Old English *faer* is akin to Old High German *fara* and Middle High German *vare,* meaning ambush, evil intent. It occurs to me that a person caught in an ambush might react by turning tail and running. And be called a coward.

I'm thinking of the fight-or-flight response, a biological survival mechanism that kicks in automatically when we find ourselves in dangerous situations. To get a quick sense of this response, imagine driving to an important meeting, or to see a friend with whom you have been arguing. You are hurrying to keep your appointment. Up ahead, the traffic light turns yellow. You know that if you run the light, you'll be on time for your meeting. It is really important to be on time. You press down the accelerator and speed through the light, which by now has turned red. You breathe a sigh of relief. Until, in your rearview mirror, you see the lights on top of a police cruiser flashing. You pull over to the curb. Caught.

If you have let yourself enter the imagery, you may notice a couple of bodily changes. Your breathing is quick and shallow. Your heart is racing. Your whole body feels energized, ready for action. If so, you are experiencing the fight-or-flight response right now. It kicked in automatically in response to the imagery.

The fight-or-flight response arises in dangerous situations. And in situations perceived as dangerous. Your imagination can kick it in, as we just saw. This is very interesting. The fight-or-flight response kicked in for me twenty years ago on Halloween. Body symptoms, such as rapid heartbeat and shallow breathing, told me that I was in danger. Of dying. Of my world falling apart. If a charging rhino attacks a caveman, he can use the energy provided by this response to jump into a tree. But where could I jump?

Everywhere I moved, the fear came with me. The isolation. The possibility of ambush. I was sinking into a state of chronic fight-or-flight, or constant vigilance against a danger I couldn't see. Even the wonderful care I got from my friends wasn't enough. I know I'm repeating myself, but I think this is important. Not until someone said to me in a way I believed, "I understand. I've been there" was I even reachable. And then that cross reached me.

Bear with me here. Bear my cross with me again. That crazy cross, as I've been calling it, touched my dread. Stopped, for that moment, the terror, the fear of ambush. And gave me a way to confront the terror when it returned. One night I squeezed it so hard while I slept that I woke up with its shape imprinted on my palm.

The cross itself wasn't enough. I now had another human being I could call who understood, who recognized the magnitude of my fear. This is not intended to belittle my friends' efforts. I love them for sticking with me. For sitting up nights with me. For confronting *their* need for help with me. For finding help for me. For pointing me toward someone who knew what I was talking about, what I was caught in. Who himself managed to be sitting in his office talking to me twenty years after something similar had happened to him.

It was being with a person who could enter my isolation that freed the power of the cross to help me. There is a secret hidden in that. An incarnational secret. We need an other to picture the deepest truths if we are to be touched by these truths. The other brings the truth, carries it, makes it possible by incarnating. "Do you see me? I'm still here. The cross protected me. I didn't explode." That's what the professor's presence said to me. His arrival in my isolated place opened me to the truth he claimed of the cross. Which, in turn, opened me to the Presence greater than the nothing that was killing me. And, unlike this sentence, it happened in an instant.

WE ARE THE MYSTERY

I notice that I feel better now. More comfortable. I sense that I am speaking with strength now. I simply can't talk about Christ in the abstract. There is no life in that for me. That is why church has so often been frustrating and empty for me. Why it didn't touch me. Why I didn't enter into the mystery. I didn't know how. Maybe this is one of the Church's big failures. Its insistence that people enter its mystery rather than finding a way to enter theirs.

We are all mysteries. We are mysteries to ourselves, if my experience as a Halloween man and as a listener has any accuracy. It is a profound mystery to me, a wonderful mystery, that when I got so lost, I got founder than I was lost. Do you see what I mean?

We need to be met where we are. The mystery is empty if it doesn't touch our isolation. This is the kind of evangelism I believe in. Going to others and entering their isolation with them. I'm thinking of my "first communion" again. That priest entered my sense of unworthiness, stepped into my world, said, "Here, this is for you. This is here for you. This exists because of lost people like you. If there weren't such lost people, we wouldn't need to bother with this."

I went to communion. I learned something that day that I finally put into practice in the past year. More than fifteen years later. Sometimes I'm a slow responder.

When I am struggling with some part of myself, when I have come to understand it a little better, or am suffering with it, I bring it to communion with me. For example, I have brought my hostile person to communion, and the one who resents my family, even the one who doesn't believe in communion, who thinks the whole thing is nonsense and hates it. It is a powerful experience to receive the bread for the hateful one, for the one who yells at Christ, "This whole thing is a lie." That is the Voice of Aloneness.

Even the Voice of Aloneness is welcome at communion. That amazes me. The coward is welcome at communion, too. In his terror of being ambushed. The one who is embarrassed to call himself a Christian is welcome.

WE ARE CHRIST

I sense another mystery here. I am feeling it now in my comfort, and enthusiasm.

I think of Jesus' words that say, in effect, "When you feed the hungry, when you give water to the thirsty, when you visit the imprisoned, when you clothe the naked, you do this for me. And when you ignore these suffering people, you are ignoring me."

When you ignore anyone, including yourself, you are ignoring Christ. Isolating Christ. Cutting yourself off from Christ. It is hard to be that naked, thirsty, imprisoned one. To be the desperately needy one. The isolated one with no clue how to connect to someone else. According to Jesus' words, as I understand them, I am Christ in need when I am so lost. I am Christ calling out to you for help. When you feed me, and give me clothes, you are doing this to Christ.

This is wild. What we've got is a Christ at the crossroads, a beaten up Christ lying in the road. A starving Christ holding out her empty bowl. A murdering Christ locked away in prison. A despairing, disbelieving, depressed Christ. An atheist Christ. Are we big enough to open to this? To see Christ in our enemies? In Saddam Hussein? In the skinny, delirious man dying of AIDS? In the one who has caused our financial ruin? Or destroyed our family? Is it even possible to see Christ there?

That, I'm afraid, is the good news. The broken one is Christ standing before us. The moaning one dying in bed is Christ lying

before us. The homeless one is Christ staring at us. Christ is everywhere. The opportunity to encounter Christ is before us and inside
us. Christ is occupying all the isolated spaces. Are we ready to open
to deeper life, the kingdom of heaven, to use Jesus' words? The
reign of God?

Where am I going with this? Perhaps a few steps further along the
way in hell. Do you see the possibilities? We have ready access to
Christ at all times. All we have to do is turn to a starving one, or
share our own starving one with another.

THE MYSTERY OF COMPASSION

Jesus did an amazing thing. Words are getting slippery now for me.
I don't know if I can capture what I want to say. I need a virginal
attitude. I need to be like that kid who ended up on Jesus' lap. That
kid opened up Christ to the world. Or like Jesus when his buddy
Lazarus died. When Jesus arrived at Lazarus' grave, he was overcome and wept with compassion. "From the bowels," to use the
literal meaning of the Greek word in the text.

Compassion is our roadway. Feeling passion with, feeling the
suffering of another. Identifying with the suffering of the other.
Stepping fully into that suffering and out of our own concerns for
just a moment. Meeting Christ.

The mystery of this is that helping the broken one helps the
helper, too. By opening the helper beyond *her* isolation. By showing her the Christness at the heart of reality. That Jesus pointed to.
As though he said, "Hey, folks! I've found the way! The reign of
God is everywhere! It's in the middle of that guy's misery. And that
little girl's tears. It's in that widow's loss, as her husband is buried.
And in that wedding feast. Look! Do you see it? Will you give yourself to it?"

Will you give yourself to it? Am I presenting something that
excites you? What if Christ, the Human One, *is* everywhere? Even
in your isolation? Even in my cowardice?

I want to say, "Amazing." Imagine. For several days, I have
struggled to write *about* Christ. I can't do it. I can't show you Christ
analytically. I want to say, "That's not where Christ hangs out." But
I may be wrong. Christ may open to others in analytical thinking.
But I wander from my point. You see the problem? Struggling not

to exclude any point of view, I often lose my own. Very important insight, that. I isolate my own point of view when I *only* am taking care not to exclude others.

Now to what I find amazing. I couldn't get to Christ by talking theology. But I did by sharing my cowardice. As though I said, "See this tail between my legs? That means I'm afraid. Feeling alone and scared." By sharing that with you, my isolation was broken. And you were brought to an experience of Christ.

Martin Luther King said something that I think applies here. "We, as Christians, have a mandate to be nonconformists." We are called to see Christ in the middle of every isolation. To run toward that isolated one, or to walk carefully so as not to frighten him, to not conform to isolation. It sometimes takes only one nonconformist to break a person's isolation.

And yet, there is no guarantee that our nonconformity will succeed. Several years ago, during Mass, at the greeting of peace, I turned to the person behind me. A young man with long, dirty hair and a beard was staring at me. When I offered my hand, he shook his head vigorously, then stared at the floor. As I turned away from him, my heart was pounding. I didn't know what to do. Maybe it was another act of cowardice not to try to reach through his refusal. Maybe it was an act of respect and helped him somehow. I hope so.

Sometimes, when I am feeling shaky and isolated, I dread the greeting of peace. There is one in me who wants to cry, "There is no peace!" Who longs to flee the church building, to get away from everyone, to get lost in his isolation because he feels so alien, so inhuman. When another person turns to me—to him—and offers her hand, I want to show him to her, to ask her to do something for him. But I don't know how. It feels like a betrayal to cry out for him. Until he is ready to cry out for himself. Until then, I feel an ache. I want to help him. I can only sit near him, waiting for a sign, for Christ to open in him. Cowardice? Or fear for him? Fear that isolation will ultimately win?

No! Isolation can never ultimately win. Because Another Alone moans at the core of isolation. Forever, if necessary. Refusing to conform to isolation. That is very comforting news to my coward. It fills him with courage.

17

PASSION

Depression is a lack of passion. An emptiness of passion. It is a consuming fire burning the person's being into smoke and dust, not a creative fire that forges tools with which to plant and harvest. Or weapons to protect, defend, or conquer. Depression doesn't care. It says to hell with it. With you. With me.

Paradoxically, such depression carries great power. It changes life into hell. It pushes people into isolation. It plants seeds of hopelessness and harvests the nothing. It disables the body. Alters body chemistry. Makes taking a step an impossibility.

IMPOSSIBILITY

Impossibility is a dangerous word. It is a *fait accompli*. It makes the fact of impossibility possible. I remember being told a story about Thomas Aquinas when I was in grade school. A couple of monks, aware of Thomas' gullibility, called out to him, "Come quick! There is an ox flying through the air." He rushed to the window. No ox was flying by. In response to his anger, they asked, "How could you possibly believe that an ox was flying by? It's impossible." He answered, "I'd rather believe an ox could fly than that my fellow monks would lie to me." Getting beyond serious depression and isolation sometimes seems about as possible as an ox flying.

Depression catches people in the grip of impossibility. The grip of impossibility, interesting, paradoxical image. How can an impossible grip anything? That's the problem, isn't it?

Starting a fire was impossible until someone rubbed two sticks together. Brought two sticks into passionate relationship with each other. That last image surprises me. Jumps right into the middle of where I was going and pushes me in a different direction.

Fire comes from vigorous relationship. From rubbing two sticks together. The sexual imagery isn't lost on me. Though sexuality, as with the other passions, disappears in hell, dissolves, turns to dust and air. This is tragic because sexuality, at its best, is a servant of relationship. It opens two people to a shared interiority of passion.

But the depressed person doesn't care about that either. For isolation isn't an empty nothing. It is an active nothing. It nothings, it no-things, it dis-be's, it calls what is impossible for *it* impossible in life. It gives possibilities the name impossible, and disempowers them. Names them not and they tend to stay not.

Nikos Kazantazkis wrote in his autobiography *Report To Greco,* "I believe in a world which does not exist, but by believing it, I create it. We call 'non-existent' whatever we have not desired with sufficient strength."

LOVE'S POSSIBILITY

Creation *ex nihilo*. Bringing into being from the nothing. Like God did in Genesis, in the beginning. Begin comes from the prefix *bi,* here, plus *ginnan,* to start (something). Thus, to begin is to start here, to start something here. Creation *from* nothing.

Remember a time when you fell newly in love. Suddenly, something that hadn't existed, not only existed, but was central to your life. Drove you to act in new ways. Made the other person the central meaning of your life. Do the fires stir at all as you remember the other's face? Her way of doing things? His silly peculiarities that so endeared you to him that you felt like squealing with delight? Or are you so depressed that you feel nothing? How frightening that is! How powerfully you have moved in the other direction! For what was once central and enlivening no longer touches you. Remember the special moments you shared together. A first kiss. A surprise gift. A look of love that broke you open. Is there a quickening yet? Does passion fire you? Or am I hurting you by recalling something that has died? Pushing you further into isolation, the impossibility of trustworthy relationship?

If so, I am sorry. But I am entering your isolation. Can you name your impossibilities and see how they are limiting you? How they are locking you into your present perception of the world? How they are causing you to factor out little looks as meaningless? Do you notice when a man smiles at you? Do you negate his smile? Do you tell yourself it means nothing or that it will just bring another round of hurt and pain?

It is a daunting thing to be passionate. Many of us get so beaten down by life that it's amazing that we go on. It's amazing that the fires can stir again.

Why aren't we amazed when young people fall in love? Why do we understand it in such a small way with statements as, "The hormones are kicking in." (They are.) Or, "That's what happens at this age." (It does.) Is that the best we can do? What if we said, if we believed, that the awesome is happening yet again? What if we honored it as the mysterious movement of life, of passion being born? What then? Would we celebrate it somehow? Would we dance to the music that we hear playing? Would we re-member it in ourselves and be caught up on its wings? Would we feel the kiss of eros? The movement of God bursting into the possibility of relationship?

Awe would change our response. But the problem is precisely that we have dis-awed ourselves. We have come to see young passion as cute, sweet. Named it puppy love. Declared wisely that it isn't the real thing. Added from our own experience that it won't last. But at least they will grow from the pain of it.

Well, they will grow from the pain of it. But why not from the fact of it? What if God is the mover of passion? What if God is calling in the nothing for the new to be? What if God isn't a neatnik (look around) and wants life, and relationship, to kick into being? What if we factor out God's movement when we try to control this passion with rules?

PASSION

I'm getting a little worked up, aren't I? I'm feeling passionate. Feeling the fire that is expressing itself. That can create and destroy. I know it can do both. But is its destructive potential reason enough to avoid it, to say no to life? That seems to me a no-win response. Protect yourself by not living? No. That's wrong. I've seen too many lives laid waste by that attitude. Too many no's said to opportunities, leading people further into isolation, and depression.

I'm not proposing an all-out abandonment to passion either. But rather that we begin to reeducate ourselves. That we learn to celebrate the holy newness of life, rather than beating it to death with our negative words. "Don't do that, dear, until you're married." "That is really disgusting. Only bad girls do that."

Do what? Come alive? Is it any wonder that people get warped attitudes about passion, and act in perverse ways, when we are told how bad this powerful movement in us is?

Or, we say nothing at all. But when we ignore passion, we don't keep it from existing. We isolate it. We force it to find its own way. We don't bring it into relationship. We increase the likelihood of its poor expression. But not of its expression. For it will express itself. Maybe as depression. Where the passion turns on the person and burns him up. This is hell. To have our fires devour us. Burn us up. Burn us out. So that we cease to be. Except as a consciousness that knows it is not living, not acting, not vital. We contribute to depression by avoiding the central importance of passion. By fearing it only, rather than having a healthy respect for it.

Is it worse to have never lived, to burn up in your unexpressed passion, than to be hurt, to be hurt terribly? To be killed? To contract AIDS, the modern plague? I know people who are dying from AIDS who claim they accept the disease as better than the lives they were living before. They opened to their passion. I also know people who are heartbroken, enraged, by what AIDS is doing to their lover, their child, their friend.

I am not promoting unrelated passion. I'm arguing that the question is bigger even than AIDS. It is a question of life. By now, you know my position. I believe, and choose to believe, that something happens even in the heart of isolation, moaning if it has to, screaming and screeching if necessary, making an obnoxious pest of itself, trying to get our attention. That something, Another Alone, God, Goddess, is life. Is the life force, the life impulse, passion, the burst of being trying to be.

I also believe that Jesus saw it. Saw it happening. Felt at the center of himself something radically new. Life in a different key. Happening all around him. Passionately. If you look at his parables of the reign of God, you'll see how common are his images. Seeds, vineyards, sheep and shepherds, lost coins, family. He saw life happening not in some beyond, some afterwards, but now. He cried out the Christ message, that humanity is included in life's transformation and central to it. That humanity can see it, can call out to it. Can relate to it. Can engage it. And change it. And incarnate it.

THINKING TOO SMALL

Leap with me. I'm moving to another place. I think that people who talk about Jesus as the Son of God are thinking too small. He is much more than that. He is the one who showed me that the impossible is possible. Who reached through and exploded in the middle of the nothing. Who got to me even from that cross. That damn cross. I don't believe that the cross, that the murder of Jesus, is salvation. That isn't the connection for me.

Am I seeing that I've changed my mind? That the crazy cross didn't help me?

Of course it helped. But must we stop there? Can't there be impossibles, which we haven't yet imagined, expressing themselves? Can't life be new? Maybe that's what annoys and frightens me so much about (here I go again) fundamentalists of every ilk. They tell me, whatever they intend to say, that it's all over, all done, decided. Like science was supposed to be at the turn of the twentieth century. But then the atom cracked open. And so did science, which is now running down a whole new road. Setting off some potent explosions as it does so. Creation and destruction.

Why can't God open life further if science can? Why can't each new life be a new opportunity for God to express life? That movement in the nothing that rejects isolation as the ultimate? That chooses relationship as the deepest reality? Relationship to people, to the world, to the life moving at the middle of it all, wanting to be ever new and ever renewing?

Leap again. To that crazy cross. What touches me now, slow learner that I am, is the utter humanity of Jesus, his total faithfulness to the vision of God erupting in the middle of everyday life. That accepts a nail bashing into his wrist, rather than saying "No" to the reality he uncovered. That uncovered him. It isn't the brutality of the cross that gives me life. Or the sacrifice of his life *per se*. It is the way of being that he opens to me, suggests to me, stirs in the fires of me, that there is something so good, so God, that it is more important than his own little life.

Could it be that Another Alone was with him as he was dying? Thousands of people died by crucifixion under the Romans. It's not the fact of crucifixion that transforms the world. What is it then?

There is a new insight burning in me. I'm trying to avoid it. It's not crucifixion that transforms the world. But the fact, as I choose to name it, that God and person met utterly in that hellish place. That Another Alone truly does sit and stir in the middle of hell. Truly does enliven even there. So that the woman in the killing camp could say, "It's okay, dear. I'll die for you."

All this amazes me. Because I am a coward. I am awed by the potential of the human. By expressions of human being that I cannot imagine in my isolation. I can't even imagine making the free throw that wins the game. Admitting my cowardice opens me, opens my isolation, pushes through to the one in me who cries out, "Show me something that is good! That is worth living for."

It isn't death that is worth living for. The cross and that brave woman don't show me that. Can I find the words? Can Another Alone stir me enough to give some adequate expression of what is moving in me? Clap your hands. Tinkerbell's light is in danger of going out. Relate to Another Alone in me who is trying to moan new words from me, to you, so that I, too, might see them in sharing them with you.

THE FIRE

Confession. I don't know what I am doing. More truly, I feel open to the nothing in the middle of me. And the nothing is now full of creative fire. Is burning me. What is worth living for? What is so life that even in dying for it it comes into being? That is so relational—I'm thinking of resurrection here—that death doesn't destroy the relationship?

The embarrassed one in me is asking me to be quiet.

The shy one is secretly agreeing with him.

The Voice of Aloneness is singing the repeating song, "It's trash. It's trash. It's trash."

Do we have the audacity to be, even for a moment? Can I dare to say to Another Alone, "Show me life even if it kills me. Even if these are my last words."

Something in the midst of me is saying "Yes" in a quiet and

determined way. While all around it, voices continue to harp that I am a fool. But don't I know that already? I am a fool. So what?

Suddenly it seems to me that I'm going to say something quite orthodox, even if in an unorthodox way. Here goes. The human matters at the center of reality. The center of reality is crying out to the human, to human beings, to the being in each of us that longs to be human. Crying out to each of us, like Meg did to the echthroi, "Be! Relate! Relate to me and to each other. Because it is in relating that you come to be. Because you aren't just you. You are an opening for me to reach the other. And I am an opening for you to the other. Moan. Cry. Call. Die for each other. Live for each other."

Again, something in me begs me to fold, to be silent. Because I am a coward. Because I fear life. Because I don't know what I'm doing.

I need to admit my ignorance. I need to feel the burning in me. It isn't burning me up right now. It is creating me. I need to tell you that there is creative life in you, too. That's what I'm trying to do. I feel something dying in me as I do so. Yes. That's it, dying.

Strangely, the image comes of my daughter being born. Showing up in the world, long and skinny, face looking like a little prune. With it, the accompanying feeling of that moment, profound, that lasted until I named it. For one moment, I was standing at the center of the world. I was being shown a mystery in which I had a very small, but significant, role. There came that familiar feeling that I didn't know what I was doing. That my life was changing with this birth. I even said to one of the nurses as my wife and I left the hospital, "You are being irresponsible sending this little kid off with two people who have very little idea how to take care of her."

Maybe we're not supposed to know what we're doing. Maybe we're just supposed to relate the best we can, to learn to love a little better. To be open to the wonder of another human being, leaping out of the nothing, ready to take on the world.

With a little help from her friends.

18

RELATIONSHIP

Depression is a curse that can bless us by defeating us. By over-powering us. By breaking us free of the belief that we are able to thrive as isolated beings. By opening our isolation to the singing of Another Alone.

Singing? Yes. So it seems to me. As we rediscover our passion, we begin to hear the melody beneath the moaning. Does this make sense to you? Has this happened during our time together?

I hope it has. I have tried to portray and to explore my belief that *we* is infinitely more than *I*. That we opens me to the universe while I only opens me to myself. So that I hear the moaning of Another Alone which becomes singing when you listen to it with me.

IMAGES OF GOD

As a child I was taught that human beings are made in the image of God. If that is so, then human beings can teach us about that of which they are images. Thus, human beings show us God. Human beings are Christ, thirsty, imprisoned, naked, in need. If we isolated beings thrive when we enter relationship, what about God? Is God, Another Alone, simply being honest when God moans in the middle of us? Is there a moaning God who is desperate for relationship? Who is pothotic, insatiable? Might the longing for eternity be God's longing in us? To bring people into being, so that we and God can relate?

I find this an exciting idea. It makes for a passionate universe. An awesome universe. It makes the universe a daunting place to live. Full of infinite possibility.

Are human beings together in relationship another image of

God? An image of the possible God? The God of story who opens relationship and the universe to meaning rather than to mere randomness? The Christian doctrine of the Trinity pictures what I'm suggesting, that the heart of life is relationship.

Relationship is a great mystery. It frees us to explore our isolation in a new way. It challenges us to grow, to become more than we are. To dare to risk that we may become more isolated if we follow the relationship that calls us to be and then lose it.

Painful business life. When we are isolated, there is nothing more to lose. Except nothing itself, by opening to the moaning that can lead us to true relationship. But relationship, which is so life-giving, suddenly changes that. To have deep friendship and then to lose it is a pain beyond compare. It is, I think, like losing God.

I have sat with enough brokenhearted people over the years not to make idealistic statements about relationship. Some people, as far as we mortal beings can tell, don't make it. They fold when they lose relationship. They crumble. They fall into despair and isolation. They die.

I find in me a desire that their stories move deeper than I am able to fathom. Images come of their discovering love again. Here and now. Or, if they die, somewhere else. As a reincarnated being or as a person caught in hell who finally hears God moaning.

THE RELATIONAL UNIVERSE

My inner being tells me, my beating heart tells me, my longing tells me, that no one can be ultimately lost. If anyone is ultimately lost, then I am, too. This is not some noble notion on my part. It is my belief in a relational universe. If you are ultimately lost, then the story of the universe is a tragedy. With the final curtain, nothing. I can't stand that. I become petulant. I want to stamp my feet like a little kid and yell, "No!"

Of course, my tantrum doesn't guarantee that the world is as I need it to be. But this is the future that I'm betting on. Counting on. Begging to be true. Because I know lostness. Lostness is awful. Is excruciating. Is unimaginable as an eternity. At least to me.

Barry Lopez has written that the world is held together by two things: compassion and story. I agree with him. Compassion breaks open isolation, is an agreement to suffer with the isolated one. Story offers possibility. Says that isolation can lead to wonder. Several times I have heard people say that they would live the horrible facts of their lives again if doing so would lead to where they have come. This is a remarkable statement. It says that their suffering has become part of their stories. That shared isolation is opening them to a loving cosmos. To the universe of possibility that is greater than the chaos. When story and compassion hold the universe together, chaos can be borne.

But something in me protests. Some aspects of life are so horrid, some isolations so great, that the chaos can't be transformed. An immediate response to that wells up in me. Throw those isolations at God. Crack them open. Demand that Another Alone redeem them. Don't cover them over.

A man who comes to me for therapy offered an image that speaks to this. Whenever anything difficult arose in his childhood family, his mother quickly plastered over it. Instantly smoothed it out so no one could see that it was there. Hid the problem behind her perfect plastering. Disappeared it. Nothinged it. Problem, what problem? But it didn't work. By denying the difficult things of life in this way, she told her son a story about the nature of the universe. She taught him that much of life can't be handled directly and openly.

He learned his lesson well. For years and years, he has hidden difficulties behind that wall of plaster. Which has inhibited relationship in his marriage and left his wife feeling isolated. Only when he has been able to bash down the plaster walls has a new story begun. In which people share the difficulties of life rather than hiding them.

Every life is a story. Every way is a story. With a beginning, middle, and end. Many of us have at least some say in how our stories go. We can change our stories, imagine the fulfilling stories of our lives. A starving child suddenly appears as a picture in my mind. As a protest, I think, against any easy claim that we can all change our stories. I am staring into the empty bowl of that child. Who is caught in a bigger story. Who embodies the results of negation. Of isolation. His eyes tell me a story of emptiness, of despair, and of something deeper still. His eyes are burning me, opening my hunger. When I look at him, I am looking at myself.

I hunger for a universe that makes sense. For a universe that desperately needs me, and the people I love. A universe that agrees with me that the people I love have ultimate significance. These little mortal creatures. Little specks of dust in the enormous universe. Who live but a minute and then are gone.

But gone where? If life is a journey, if we are, as physicist Paul Dessauer claimed, *in statu viatoris*, that is, creatures of the way, wanderers, then perhaps earth is part of our journey. Perhaps a *necessary* part of our journey. Perhaps the story of our lives is this: We are born to embody ourselves. To incarnate as images of God. To become human beings who grow into the awesome possibility of equal relationship with God. Because God is lonely and groaning without us and within us. Is the most needy one in the whole universe. We are thus invited to enter isolation, where God is. To be changed into relational creatures rather than isolated ones. Not broken branches soon to die, or drops soon to return to the cosmic Oneness. But *ex nihilos* called to be. Anti-echthroi. Matters. Mattered creatures who matter.

I remember giving a talk a couple years ago at a church on the humanity of Jesus during which it occurred to me that his perspective, and the Christian perspective as I understand it, can be said in two words: Matter matters. That is a lovely sentence. A tautology. Noun and verb sharing the same space. Matter matters. Matter comes from *mater*, mother. Matter is the mother of us all. I am filled with excitement by that thought. Matter is the mother of us all. We are here, so my story goes, to be born. To incarnate. To embody. And not as isolated critters, but as relational ones.

As lovers. Passionate beings. Love. Let's ponder love together. Let's enter into love together. Is that okay with you? Does it foster fantasies, memories perhaps, of the hurt of love? Of love's emptiness, of its broken promise?

Then shout that out! Don't hide it. Scream at love for letting you down. I don't want you to be stuck in isolation. And I am cheering you on as you voice and moan and shout your fury at love gone bad.

Or maybe love hasn't been terrible to you. Maybe it just hasn't been there. Then demand it to come. Don't go easy with love. If it's worth its salt then it will come. Some way. I remember talking with a lonely woman whose life has been empty of the love she deserves. She was sharing her despair of ever finding love. An idea came to me that I fired out quickly. Usually, I let such thoughts go by. And they fall, I'm afraid, into the abyss of loneliness. I said to her (she's a religious woman), "Demand that God show you relationship after you leave here, before you get home." She called me right after she arrived home and said, "It happened three times on my way home." One of those times was simply a smile from a man on the subway train.

Simply? No, no, no. *Transformatively* a smile. *Relationally* a smile. The universe saying to her, you matter. And more important than the universe, another human being.

You heard me right. Thus goes my story. Human beings are more important than the universe. Something in me is protesting again. I can't mean that a little mortal from Milwaukee or Minneapolis or Marlborough, Massachusetts is more important than the stars.

But that's how it seems to me. But comparisons are odious. More truly, we tend to miss the eternal importance of the human being. If matter matters, then what becomes matter in specific form is matter's expression of its story. Do you follow me?

This woman was met in her loneliness. Three times. And the universe changed for her in some small, significant way.

I remember another time listening to her struggle with her loneliness. I could think of nothing to say to help her escape it. Or to share it with her. I suggested to her that we stop, that we close our eyes and sit quietly for a few minutes. Again, something transformative occurred. When she opened her eyes she said with deep feeling, "No one has ever sat quietly with me before." Shocking, sad statement. Another hungry child with an empty bowl.

19

DEPARTURE

Time comes now for our paths to diverge. A feeling of sadness touches me. You have listened to my story. Have shared Halloween and the new life that has followed after it. You have watched me open to my cowardice and find a world of relationship and hope there.

Will you take a few things with you as you go? Will you remember that there is another person who believes that isolation isn't ultimate? That depression is the cry of your soul to open beyond isolation to the mystery that resides within you and between us? That you aren't the only show in town? That the Voice of Aloneness, like Mephistopheles, if you will listen, is the first statement of the reality of your inner being? But not the final statement of your valuelessness. Will you also remember Another Alone? You can call Another Alone Goddess, Goddy, Great Spirit, God. But know that Another Alone is right in the middle of you, in your depression, moaning in your isolation. Will you remember imagination, that is full of possibilities that can bring you beyond your isolation?

Will you take a step beyond your isolation and help another broken one? Feed a hungry one? Hug a despairing one? Wail with someone who has lost her child, her lover, her job?

We are given a choice. We can serve isolation. We can be racists, sexists, classists. Or we can serve relationship.

Two years after Halloween, I was living in downtown Boston, teaching in a federal program. Kids from the inner city and from the suburbs were brought together to use the city as a classroom. And to get to know each other as human beings. At first, I was quite a good teacher. I involved the kids, got them relating to one another. Helped them get involved in creative projects. But something went dead in me. I realized that I didn't know what I was doing. I wasn't finding my life, wasn't serving the deeper hunger that was in me. And I was becoming a poor teacher—a babysitter, not a catalyzer. As I walked home one day, feeling lost and confused, and worried about the future, I turned the corner and stepped onto the street where I lived. A large black man was walking toward me with his head down. As he drew near to me, he lifted his head, caught my eye, and smiled. Like that guy did on the subway. I felt my isolation and confusion melt away. I smiled back at him. For a moment, I was looking at Christ. And so was he. That's what it's all about, I think. Stepping out of our own isolation and into the isolation of the other.

BEGINNINGS

There is life beyond depression. There is relation and opening to God. For everyone. *Everyone*. That is the deepest demand of a relational universe. Everyone, even you, even I, is included.

Can we see depression as a beginning toward relating compassionately to the world? What happens when we do that? Does the universe shift for us? Does life become possible again?

A woman who has fought depression all her life (and fought it well) recently told me a dream. In her dream, the landscape was utterly destroyed. Fire had consumed everything as far as her eye could see. As she walked through the desolation, she came upon a small hole in which rested a container full of fire. Joy filled her at the realization that the fire hadn't destroyed itself. That *creative* fire remained.

Paradox. The fire that utterly destroys is hell. The fire that forges and strengthens and gives hope is life.

I am reminded of the play *J.B.* by Archibald MacLeish, a modern rendering of the story of Job. At the end of the play, as they move among the ruins, J.B. and his wife Sarah are clutching one another. J.B. says, "It's too dark to see." And Sarah answers, "Then blow on the coal of the heart, my darling." "The coal of the heart," he repeats. She replies, "It's all the light now." Is this a recipe for despair? Or is it a cry of hope even at the center of nothingness?

Beginning means seeing where we are and then taking one step. If the "coal of the heart" is the only hope, blow on it. If the land of your life is utterly destroyed, come before that contained fire. Let it burn you. Let it enliven you.

A promise. The end is never the end. There is always an imaginative step to take no matter how awful the awful is. As T. S. Eliot says, "In my end is my beginning." Yes. If you have walked this far with me, dare to believe that even at the heart of your darkness, God is always beginning, always starting, always moaning, always new inside you. Longing to draw you into loving relationship with the world.

Understand that depression is ultimately a hypothesis about the world. A body belief that isolation reigns. Depressed people who test this hypothesis to its core often come to the conclusion that the nothing is the ultimate. It isn't. That is my operating principle. The nothing isn't ultimate. Every little image defies the nothing. Rejects it. Longs to lead us to our beginning.

Open to the images that are in you. Share them with a trusted friend. Take the next step. Each step can be the beginning. A step out of hell and into life.

SUGGESTED READINGS

I want to suggest a few pertinent books to the interested reader. Contained in these books are bibliographies, should you want to pursue any area further.

ON THE IMAGINATION

Hillman, James. *A Blue Fire*. New York: Harper Collins, 1989.
An anthology of Hillman's books. Hillman writes as passionately as anyone I know on the world of imagination and its reality.

Kelsey, Morton T. *The Other Side of Silence*. Mahwah, N.J.: Paulist Press, 1976.
Adventure Inward. Minneapolis: Augsburg, 1980.
Companions on the Inner Way. New York: Crossroad, 1983.
These three books provide a practical guide to developing the imagination. For those who are not familiar with Kelsey, I suggest beginning with *Adventure Inward*.

Progoff, Ira. *At a Journal Workshop: The Basic Text and Guide for Using the Intensive Journal Process*. New York: Dialogue House, 1975.
Gives various exercises demonstrating many possible methods for encountering one's inner images.

ON OTHER CAUSES OF DEPRESSION

Gold, Mark S. *The Good News About Depression: Cures and Treatments in the New Age of Psychiatry*. New York: Villard Books, 1987.
Covers the landscape of the many physical causes of depression.

ON THE HEALING POWER OF LOVE

L'Engle, Madeleine. *A Wind in the Door*. New York: Dell, 1973.
Luke, Helen M. *Dark Wood to White Rose*. New York: Parabola Books, 1989.
Lynch, James J. *The Broken Heart*. New York: Basic, 1977.
   The Language of the Heart. New York: Basic, 1985.
   On the power of the hidden language of the heart that can kill and heal us.

FOR INSPIRATION IN THE IMPOSSIBLE STRUGGLE

Havel, Vaclav. *Disturbing the Peace*. New York: Vintage, 1991.
Hillesum, Etty. *An Interrupted Life*. New York: Pantheon, 1983.